Mexico
Returns

Bob White

Mexico Returns

by Mexico Returns

Illustration
By Bob White
http://www.bobwhitestudio.com/

Cover Artwork
By Brad McMinn
http://www.southernwaterdesigns.com/

Woolly Bugger Press — Winston-Salem

The contents of this book have been collected and archived from the Drake Magazine's bulletin board; http://www.drakemag.com, by Kevin Symes, aka Fatman.

We are thankful for the wonderful community of miscreant fly fishermen, Old Dog, AftonAngler, Veeetch, Jerome, mikeo, Bait for Bitches, southernstrain, Lenny, D. Micus., JRH, Tx., Midstream, flyman241, Snapdad, Woolybug25, Alteredstates, NICH, Ajax16, fishnut08, VAKU, Old Dog, Jed, TroutBumReinke, and many others who take the time to post entertaining trip reports, inane questions and thought provoking material. Thanks, especially to Mexico for his intriguing, informative and humorous replies. These post were made between February 15, 2008 and January 8, 2016.

A portion of the proceeds from the sale of this book go to The Bonefish and Tarpon Trust, to help support their mission: To conserve and restore bonefish, tarpon and permit fisheries and habitats through research, stewardship, education and advocacy.

http://www.bonefishtarpontrust.org/

The typeface used is Adobe Caslon Pro, Caslon is a group of serif typefaces designed by William Caslon I (1692–1766), and various revivals thereof. Caslon shares the irregularity characteristic of Dutch Baroque types. It is characterized by short ascenders and descenders, bracketed serifs, moderately high contrast, robust texture, and moderate modulation of stroke.

For Deborah Harry, D. Scott Deal, Mark Krowka, Mike Myatt, Butch Constable and anyone who ever whiffed an easy cast or threw out a gork that got lunched. May the tides be with you, the wind and sun at your back and the fish coming slow and true.

Mexico Returns

"No eternal reward will forgive us now for being wasted at dawn."
--Mexico Morrison

"I'd rather have a bottle in front of me than a frontal lobotomy."
--Steve Martin

"It's not that life is short, it's just that you're dead for so long."
--BoBo The Clown

Contents

Introduction
by way of the Drake

I t's been noted here that newbies sometimes get a rough treatment. Here is one response, written by Old Dog, that might help those thinking of making their first post understand a little bit about this place. After you read this take a moment (or two or three) and look around and get a sense of this place. If you're still interested make your intro and join the fray. —Jed

"This is the Drake Message Board. It is not the Drake Magazine. Tom Bie is the editor of The Drake Magazine, and this is his website, but Tom lets this message board run by a different set of rules, it is not your typical fly fishing message board, and not for the faint of heart. If you want to tell Tom how much you like the magazine, send him an e-mail, don't post here.

This is not your local fly shop. This is the fly shop an hour after it closes. The sports are gone and the whiskey's been opened for a while. There may even be a bong making the rounds. These guys are either blowing off steam from the day or getting ready to hit the water tonight. Either way, don't expect to just walk in and be welcomed with open arms. You can put up a trip report or something to show them what you got, or you can just sit and listen, you might learn something. But you can't expect someone to pass you the pipe when they don't know anything about you.

Imagine you and three friends are on a two day float. The two guys who own the boats, rowed all day, reminded you how to cast, unknotted your leader, and put you on fish were recommended by a local. They probably don't have a web page and surely don't keep a twitter updated, they fish. When you make camp, they have their own tent and fire. This board is their fire. Don't pull up a seat unless you're invited to stay. You may see and hear things you don't want to hear, and it may not be about fishing at all.

At the Drake, don't let your kids or your girlfriend open the owner's gear locker on the boat. They won't find the latest issue of Fly Fishing magazine; they are likely to find an old Penthouse and some beer.

There are decades of experience here on the Drake board. If you want to learn something, pull up a chair and listen! Use the search button or read the original version of the AK Chronicles. Do not just jump in and expect them to give you the last cold beer.

This board is a dysfunctional family of brothers, cousins, and uncles (with a few sisters and aunts). Who else would drive 10 hours to fish where they have never been with a half dozen guys they don't know. Even offer to pick up someone they have never met to go along for the ride. It's an obsession with fly fishing and its mutual respect. Some of these folks have been on this board since it ran so slow you could log on, light a cigar and get a beer before the damn thing loaded. You had to survive long enough to make 50 posts before they would let you have an avatar.

When you think you are ready, put together a trip report and introduce yourself with pictures, and through in some BP&P to entertain the crowd. Don't try to impress anyone with your words until you've brought something to share at the fire." —Old Dog

Road Trip

Ultimate Roadtrip
AftonAngler

12 months

*Mine – May to May, start in Wisconsin, end in Wisconsin, other than
that I can go anywhere that will let me in, no more than four hours
of driving allowed before a mandatory fishing stop must be executed...*

*Goal to explore angling in the way it was meant to be done. My
American dream = a year in my RV just letting the fishing spirit move
me about the cabin...free to roam, free to fish, sleep when you are tired,
eat when you are hungry.*

*Meet people from all walks of life. Sponge off of em for a spell and move
on.*

Think about it.

*I'd start out on my 40th birthday in mid May (great birthday present
really eh?). Prolly down at Little Whiskey...my Camp in the driftless...
spend a week or so milking that and then I'd move into a low grade orbit
that would take me roughly around the upper Great Lakes...*

MEXICO RETURNS

Who knows…maybe that would take the entire summer…then maybe head out to the east coast and on down south…maybe head out west and go down the coast…

Definitely would not be up here in December/Jan/Feb/March…

When I was just a kid I saw a great slide show by Tom Anderson that revolved around what he would do if he had 12 months free to fly fish… not a road trip mind you…his was a pie in the sky type of thing… inspired me though…

I'll argue that we all have 12 months free to fly fish. It's just that we put road blocks up and make excuses on why we can't/won't do it. Think outside the box.

I already did my undergraduate studies in this mind you. Was in a deal for Fly Rod & Reel back in 2004 called the Trout Bum Tournament… fuckers gave me $500 and had me stay out as long as the money would last…should have been the Champion…only that year the pricks decided it would be cool/PC to name the winning team based on how much $$$ they could raise for a charity…

That part sunk me. Other than that I rolled for 22 glorious daze and hit the shit like it was on sale brothers and sisters. Fished all over Wisco., MN, Mich. – upper and lower, Ont.Canaida…bummed a free ride across Lake Mich. On the SS Badger…did side trips to St. Croix Rod factory, Harris Reels…gave a fly fishing seminar for Big Brother Big Sisters program and gave em some donated fly fishing tackle…

Caught tons of shit…troots, bass, panfish, muskie, suckers…stepped on some Gobies heads for some little girls over in Mitchigan…they thought I was Jesus Christ until I did that…

Ahmen!

I am seriously considering this. And I am not kidding… How would you do it?

Travel the country...eating roadkill and berries...crapping standing up...wiping your butt like the bears... fishing like a fool and feeling like a fool... little square of hash in your pocket wrapped in foil in case Barney shows you his one bullet and asks for I.D...You can hand him the foil and say, "I don't have my wallet officer, but I'm sure this silver bullet ought to prove I'm the Lone Ranger...

Get you a sign that says "Hand Jobs $10, Cheese samwiches $2...you'll never go hungry...

Dogs are good... big fucking dogs... keep you warm, safe, and you can eat them if you need to... If the neighbors get snoopy on ya, all they need is to step in a turd the size of Wyoming to send them packing...Give them the old Afton Brown Foot... No need to wash clothes... just grab them off the clothes lines you cross...So you're not big on paisley...Fuck man, it goes with jeans...

You'll want photographic evidence... Cruise the country clubs and crash the weddings... load up on cake, nail a bridesmaid, grab the disposable cameras off the tables...be sure to shoot some nudies of the bridesmaid for the couple's album...you can mail them later...

Shit, this is sounding good already... I'm in!

Boob Jobs

What to do when she wants to get her tits done?
Veeetch

*Not that I would really take anyone's advice from the suck, but what is
the best strategy when dealing with a young woman who has encountered
such a dilemma? Surely, there are wise ones amongst our ranks who will
chime in....*

I've had relationships with two women that have had the surgery...
One did it because she was so flat, she felt like a boy, and she
had the personality that it kind of freaked her out afterwards
that everyone was staring at her rack all the time...The other did
it because she wanted the world to stare at her rack...So obviously
there were different motives here...

The first was a wholesome, all American girl who got a boob job
to improve her self image, and in the end she became a stripper/
sneeze queen that left her husband (not me) for another woman...
The second flared out just about any time I even looked at another
woman, despite the fact that I was always getting into fights
because of the way she dressed to attract attention then when she
got it would react ambiguously, one time smiling and attracting an

aggressive response I'd have to shut down and the next time just grabbing the nearest beer off the bar, stuffing her thumb in the top, shaking it and spraying down the guy hawking her, pissing him off and the person who belonged to the beer...She eventually became a stripper, and now lives with another woman...

So to conclude my personal observations, implants lead to flare out, nude dancing and lesbianism...With that in mind, it's up to you...

Traveling Cross-Country

Fishing Cross the Cuntry.....
Jerome

Will be heading for Ga from Idaho next week...

Driving unfortunately could not be avoided.

So i am looking to you guys for ideas and suggestions on making the most out of it and making it a hell of alot more interesting...

Seeing that my fly fishing and music are about my only interests in life anymore, why not fish as much as possible for whatever is available to a wade fisher making the drive..... or if any of you want to take my lame ass fishing....

and I will document this it as well and amusingly interesting as possible for you losers on the suck.... in my own lame way of course..

so fire away please....

otherwise go fuck yourself and die.... please...

Ahhhhhh----FUCK!...Where do I begin...Like Idaho, Georgia is home to misguided mountain youths who like to believe their college football teams are worthy of their rankings, yet a season of fall Saturday muckety-mucks rubs a proverbial turd under their noses...

So invoking the rights of true southern hospitality, methinks you should avoid states like Texas, Oklahoma, Alabama and Florida on your jaunt, if for no other reason than to have to take a beatdown from a rodeo clown...After all, Georgia is where the toothbrush was invented, otherwise it would have been named the "teethbrush"...

Now you should be safe traversing Utah, Colorado and Wyoming, but expect your presence in Nebraska and Kansas to draw some hurtled epitaphs and the occasional "Potato in the Tailpipe"... The real grist of your trip will be east of those areas, as you hit Missouri, a state with a bucket of bees up their ass and a buzz of indignation...Alas a detour south is pointless as the closer you get to the Oklahoma border, the more hair will fall off your butt...

So that means another northerly migration, and a slow roll into more liberal ideologies as you circle through Iowa and Illinois... Expect more misguided retribution in Indiana, but just shake off that crap as a bad religious sacrifice...The real threat and probably your biggest obstacle will come as you enter Ohio, where it's easier to find a coaching staff with a volatile temper than an opponent with a winning record, and despite marked pastings in bowl games, the gentry refuses to believe that having more than one good team to play annually helps establish a solid argument for a single #1 vote...

You might also consider skirting the borders of Kentucky and Tennessee, although down in talent this year, they will require you to pass a written exam before they will let you:

A.) Howl at their wimmen; B.) Drink real Bourbon or Sour Mash from a dirty jar; C.) Shoot an animal and let you pork their woman on top of the still warm carcas: or D.) Call out Hank Williams Jr.

as a husk of his father's talent...The test usually consists of donning antlers and a taupe fur coat, and zipping through the woods on a bicycle with a grunt tube duct taped between your butt cheeks...

The jaunt south through West Virginia, Virginia, North and South Carolina should be limited in its pain, although I'd suggest avoiding the subjects of barbeque sauce, pig farms, Oysters Rockefeller and hair on the palm of your hand...Oh, and a couple of other things... When you stop at gas station to take a piss, don't eat the rock candy in the urinal, cause it ain't worth a shit!...and be sure your nuts have dropped before you pick up a can of dip and stuff a little wad of freshness into your bottom shelf, cause you'll spend half a day on the side of the road lying in red clay and laughing at the leaves...

As for fishing...If it looks wet, why not wave your rod around in it?... Loss of accent isn't enough...You have to pass this test before your soul can be purified and you can once again stare at a sports rag sans feelings of discontent....

Here's the test...

You have to be in Georgia...Pick a shitty little bar, I could really care less which, there's certainly no lack of options...Have a buddy walk in, belly up, and ask the bartender loudly what's with the big red and black "G" on all the hats and trucks?...

The bartender will likely respond, "Why that's the Georgia Bulldogs!"…

Your buddy follows it up with, "Georgia Bulldogs?...You sure are proud of an animal that looks more at home on the floor of a butcher shop than in the woods, why shoot you even dress your kids up in little cheerleader outfits all because of some slack jawed mutt..."

The bartender will clarify the misunderstanding with, "No son, The Georgia Bulldogs, You know the University of Georgia Football Team..."

To which your buddy responds... "get the fuck outta here, Georgia has a football team?"...

Then the test...You have to keep him from getting his eyes closed for good...

Newbie

Please Let Me Introduce Myself
mikeo

POST DELETED

*This follows an initial post that Canadians are proof that Indians
fucked buffalo that spun the thread poster out and sent him on a rant,
followed by requests that the forum moderator punish those making
racial remarks... The Rant from the original poster is in capital letters,
the true meaning defined afterwards by Mexico Returns.*

It really can't be this easy, can it?...First off, I'm fucking pissed at
you fucks...After taking my stab and watching the flare out, I
came in to work this morning and read the entire thread...Do
you have any idea how much it hurts to blow a yogurt smoothie
through your nose?...It's like...like...hearing no one wants to read
your story even though you spent countless hours with your face
in a thesaurus translating Indian terms to Queen's English and
closing your eyes to vividly capture a scene on paper...And all that
other crap your English 101 teacher told you to do...

But alas, I feel my initial comments might have been too abrasive,
and quite possibly insulting to American buffalo, so it is with

umbrage that I respond to my Canindian friends commentary within...

mikeo wrote:
REALLY WISH I COULD SAY THIS HAS BEEN FUN --Or at least as enjoyable as taking my girlfriend Cody Tatonka to the mall for her Glamor shots...

BUT IF NOTHING ELSE I'LL CHALK IT UP TO EXPERIENCE -- So this is what you mean by catching instead of pitching...

I HAVE DELETED MY FIRST TWO POSTS -- I'm taking my ball and going home, and you meanies can just live in Meanieville without me, cause you won't have this Canindianalo to kick around any more...

I WON"T BE POSTING HERE ANY MORE -- Cause MikeO is an Indian term meaning "No self esteem"...

IF THIS IS SUPPOSED TO BE THE "REAL" FLY FISHING FORUM THEN YOU ALL NEED TO GET A GRIP ON REALITY -- Cause I'll bet some of your signatures aren't even your "Real" given name...

I MAY NOT HAVE COME ON HERE PROPERLY PREPARED BUT THESE "WELCOMING" RESPONSES FROM EVERYBODY HAS BEEN LESS THAN EXPECTED -- Okay, so I'm a dumbass, but you're not supposed to call me out on that...you...you...Hooligans...

I DON'T WANT TO STOOP TO THE LEVEL OF THE POSTS I SEE HERE -- Since I have no witty comebacks that I can think of right now...But you wait until later...later, I'm going to get you good...

AND I'VE STARTED TO THROW BACK SOME OF THE SAME CRAP AS I RECEIVED -- See, it's later, here, take a

bite of this shit burger...I mean burger...haha....no really, it's good..
see, I'll even take a bite...Hahaha...it's filled with shit, you crazy fly
fishing knownothings...

NOT MY STYLE -- Cause I'm more into self prescribed accolades
and fur-lined underwear as opposed to depricating commentary
and flip flops...

AND NEITHER IS THIS BOARD -- See, I've got my ball, and
you don't...hahahaha...I'm walking away...don't bother to ask me
to come back...cause I won't...here I go...I'm walking...I'm getting
farther away...And I have my ball...

QUITE FRANKLY ALL I SEE IS A BUNCH OF JUVENILE
DELIQUINT WANNABES THINKING IT'S COOL TO BE
COME ACROSS AS PSEUDO INTELLECTUALS -- So take
that...You...you...psuedos!!!...

POSERS IS BEST PHRASE I CAN THINK OF -- That no one
has already used to make fun of me...

NOTHING GENUINE HERE -- Or at least no gratuitous
applause for my essay writing skills...I also have bow hunting skills...
numbchuck skills...

NO REAL SUBSTANCE --And STOP calling me Napoleon!...
Geesh...you stupidnicks...

NOT IN WHAT I SAW POSTED IN RESPONSE TO MY
INTRO (NO MATTER HOW POORLY IT WAS RECEIVED
NOBODY HAS THE RIGHT TO FLING THE SHIT
AROUND LIKE I'VE SEEN FLUNG HERE) -- It sucks when
you forget your shit screen and bullshit repellant...

SO I POSTED MY "INITIATION" PICS -- HUH?... SO
WHAT --Laugh if you want, but Cody's fur keeps me warm on
those cold winter nights, while you dumb fucks will be stuck trying
to warm yourself against the ass of a naked woman...Stupid fucking

Americans...Who's the idiot now?...

BIG DEAL, WHO REALLY CARES --I mean, besides me...

I DON'T -- And neither does Cody...

AND I SEE NOTHING WORTH MY WHILE REMAINING ON HERE OR WORTH MY TIME GETTING INTO A BUNCH OF B.S FLINGING -- Really guys...I'm leaving...I've got my ball...Guys?...

SO I'LL STICK TO THE OTHER FORUMS -- Where it's acceptable to be a Canindianalo lover...

IF THEY'RE THE "FAKE" ONES, THEY SEEM MORE REAL TO ME THAN THIS ONE DOES -- Here, pinch my nipple..feel that...it's real...now pinch this teat..feel that..real...I don't have to bow to your silicone mountains and platinum tongue studs because I know that real women don't trim their fur...

KEEP YOUR LINES WET and REMEMBER: "No matter how complicated life can get -- remember life is sometimes like fly fishing; after turning over every rock in the river trying to "match the hatch", you have probably spooked every fish for miles" -- Just remember this, not matter how much you utilize overused phrases, He who goes to bed with itchy butt, wakes up with smelly finger... so don't let the "little things" BUG you -- Like they've bugged me and driven me out of my mind, running screaming... ahhhhhhhhhhhhhhhhhh.....Hey, who has my ball?...just enjoy whatever you find."

I'LL SEEK MY ENJOYMENT WHERE THERE'S LESS HASSLE OR BULLSHIT TO DEAL WITH.--Oh, here's my ball...I'm really going now...I mean it this time...I'm leaving, and I'm not coming back...And I'm taking my ball...That's right, I'm taking the ball...And going...and...

Personally I could give a shit about what anybody on this board thinks --

MEXICO RETURNS

Which is why I haven't commented or reacted in any way...So there...put that in your peace pipe and smoke it...

could care less if you like my writing or not -- Really, I'm not offended at your comments about my writing, it's the fact that you wouldn't read it at all that makes me want to grab a bag of balloons, stick a funnel in my GF's ass and mail all of you buffalo farts for Christmas...

could care less if you like to carry on moronic sarcasm (remember sarcasm is the lowest form of wit; usually employed by those with half of one -- And only above the intelligence spectrum of those that employ silly phrases in parentheses... evident in the number of half wits here) -- Cause whole wits isn't a word...I looked it up...

and Nemo you're right I obviously didn't do my homework -- And Nemo, I HATE YOU for not immediately coming to my aid, quashing this rebellion and instituting rigorous punishments, banishments and some sense of institutional order...

guess I expected more than the crap I got -- So now I'm going to call thinskinaholicsanonymous and dime all of you fuckers out... and my concerns over racist remarks weren't about being a Canuck -- Cause everyone knows Canuck's are a rung lower on the evolutionary ladder than the French...which are just a rung lower than the Czecks...which are just a rung below fecal coliform... it was remarks about Indians and buffalo that pissed me off -- And that fucking Mexican...Hey Mexico, you mow my fucking lawn in the summer...hahahahaha....

about as proper as if somebody was to remark on how this thread seems to have proven the problems of inbreeding--You MOTHERFUCKERS!...

Anyway, Nemo says give you guys a chance -- So this Nemo guy has your back instead of mine, and says this is all a misunderstanding, that it's part of the initiation...that you guys really don't mean what you said and that it was just a lucky guess about me and my buffalo bride...

that my post was like singing Air Supply's "Making Love Out Of Nothing At All" in a Detroit black bar -- What's wrong with Air Supply...Shoot, you probably don't like ABBA either...

well, not one to make something out of nothing at all -- Well I, for one, am offended, and will show you how offended I am by using another overused phrase...

and since I was told that there is a process to follow in this initiation -- I'm diming you out Mexico...Hear me everyone...Mexico sent me a PM saying you fucks weren't being fucks, that you fucking always fucking respond to fucking first posts by fucking, fucking with the fuck...you fucks, fucks, fucks...and you too Mexico...You fucking fuck!...

first fish then boobs (hard to find any good ones of those as most were already posting on this thread) then pie (now Freud would have had a field day with the fish/T&A/pie scenario) -- In a hundred million years I would never demean myself by stooping to your sophomoric bullshit initiation process...and besides, everyone knows Canindianalo have their legs on upside down...

so here goes: Well, okay...If you're not going to chase after me and ask me to bring my ball back, then I'm just going to bring it back and let you play with it...So there!...

College Advice

Decisions, Decisions, Decisions...
Bait for Bitches

I know that a lot of bull shit flies around this board but I have been pondering something, that for some reason (which I will most likely regret), I feel like talking to you guys about.

I am a Junior in High School, and Mommy is starting to push me to look at Colleges. While I was reluctant at first, I have come to look at it as somewhat of a four-year (maybe 5 or 6) vacation. Well, fly fishing is a huge part of my life and will have a huge influence on where I go to school. And, luckily for me, my parents are cool with that. I live here in PA, but would be more than comfortable anywhere. I just need to be able to fish a solid river throughout the school year. I am self-reliant and confident, so I'd be alright away from home.... Well, I'm looking to get into something along the lines of Fisheries and Nat'l Resources Management. I wan't to go somewhere where I could major in something along those lines. Where did you guys go? Wish you would have gone? Have any input? So far Utah State University in Logan is really standing out. Logan River runs through campus. Green and Provo are close along with countless others and they have a specialty school in Nat'l Res. Management. Also, SUNY ESF in Syracuse has been one I'm looking at.

Well, this thread could get out of hand, but I'll welcome any input on any apsect of the College experience. Thanks Guys.

Mike

Okay kid, assuming you are real, I'll give you the skinny on college...First, don't get into fisheries management or anything involving fisheries, marine biology, mariculture or aquaculture unless you want to be poor...Sorry to piss in your waders, but I did four years and $45K in loans to learn that a BS in aquaculture offered: A.) a job in Belize for $6 an hour and all the cormorants I can shoot: B.) A job in Seattle for $7 an hour and all the eagles I care to photograph; or C.) A job at the local beach as a lifeguard for $9 an hour and all the women I could eat...er.. waves I could surf...

Hear that the aquaculture jobs are up to $8.50 an hour these days...

Now if you want to make a ton of money and have 2/3's of your time off to fish, be a fireman...Eat until you're tired, sleep until you're hungry, and work every third day...And I hear the school is...um... somewhat easier than the typical Grenadian Medical University...

So you might want to rethink your college major and point a course towards something computer related...At least you could end up playing a lot of video games...And keep in mind that 20 years ago, a geek couldn't get laid with a pocket full of cash, an ounce of beak and the keys to a Maserati, but today, the geeks rule the office...And because they are INSTRUMENTAL in the ability for a woman to view Match.Com, Facebook, and all her gossip sites, women know they have to suck up to you and not only be nice, but play nice too...

So now that we've got your major narrowed down, let's rethink the year-round fishing thing...The reality is that there's a buttload of places you can go and fish all year...and every fucking one of them is south of the Mason Dixon line...The fact that the farther south you go the less clothes women wear narrows your options to Florida, California, Hawaii or out of country...Might as well stay somewhere the electricity works on a regular basis...Which means California if you still want to chase trout, or Florida if you want to pursue the graduate course in casting...And might I advise that if you choose Florida, you don't opt for the Keys, unless you get married right out of HS, because to fish there, you need to be married so you're

MEXICO RETURNS

used to being denied...

That all being said...I'll throw you a couple of idioms to live by: Don't eat the rock candy in the urinal...It's not worth a shit... Women lie...It's just their way...think of them as an E-Ticket ride and move on...

There is no shame in masturbation...Is there MikeO?...

If there are two women and two of you...Mention right away that the fat chick wants your friend...

In regards to anything cold...poke it first to see if it's dead...

Just my $.02

At some point in your young life you should try to catch a fish on fly with serious balls...I don't mean something that fights hard, but something that when you set the hook, the next 15 seconds is consumed with you trying to retain possession of the rod...And the truth is, that ain't going to happen in a stream in Pennsylvania (No slight on PA, as it has its merits)...

U of M is great, and in the next few years you'll get to go to some national championship games while at the same time knocking the bottom out of the South Beach Eurotrash...

U of South Florida has four girls for every guy, which means even if you're a homely zit face you'll still get to kick it with a hottie that you can take pics of and send to your friends to rub it in...

Best of all, the Keys aren't far from either of these places...

Oh, and one more thing...It's a known fact that the average Florida college student scores with more hot babes in a single semester than an entire wall street brokerage firm does in the course of a year...So it isn't always about the money...

Bonefish

FL bones or other salties?
southernstrain

I know its shitty of me to ask this much of you guys but...for the last few months i've burnt up google on the subject

searched the forums here as well but with 60+ hits on bonefish, keys, keys bonefish its rough

see the drake bake happenin in march (possibly) unfortunately I won't be able to make it that early. looking at putting this trip together late spring...late april early may. Will have enough extra coin for about 1/2 day w/ a guide but other than that i'll be looking at tryin to rent a yak to explore the flats. Internet has been iffy (which is expected) with some sources saying diy's can be productive while others state its impossible. i figure the truth lies towards the latter with some exceptions...

Ah fuck it i'm pumped, what can i expect? lookin at shots on any fish to maximize my free time

have 8,9 and 10wt, lookin for my first salty fish

MEXICO RETURNS

L et me preface this by saying I am 0-for-Islamorada bonefish...
Part of that is the fact that when I show up the wind blows 30,
and part of it is giving the shot to an undeserving douchebag
that will break the fish off on its first run...

Long Key has some nice bones right in front of the campground...
Wade the south end at a dawn low incoming...Remember, the fish
are big, so you're not going to find them in 8 inches of water...more
like 2 feet...Anne's Beach is another good option...

It's best if you're married, so you're used to being denied...If your
fly lands anywhere near the fish, expect it to rush past the fly and
flip you off in one gesture of movement...In other words, consider
it an accomplishment if you even get near a Keys bonefish...

A reasonable expectation is that over four or five days, you might
walk where a bonefish has shit...Everything else is gravy...

Across from the Breezy Palms you'll see a clump of rocks and an
overgrown path into the woods...The path leads to an inland pond
that is full of tarpon Jr.s and the occasional homeless person...Bring
some small yellow sliders...Don't bring a woman--the bums will
want to sniff her...

Box fish, small sharks and houndfish really aren't fish...Don't even
think about casting to them or your juju will be fucked for the
entire trip...

The same goes for letting a bum sniff your lady...Whack them with
the rod tip...they'll hiss, but will back off...

Merry Christmas

Okay, seeing how it's my first Christmas with you Suck-ers...I'm going to offer up a present...My little way of saying you guys are alright in typical Mexico burnout-surfer lingo...Hope you enjoy....And I'll catch up with ya after the Holiday...Be safe, Merry little tribe...

Charlie's Pride

"How long?" asked Charlie in a low, soft voice. "Not long now. Another five or 10 minutes and we'll see the shoreline. As soon as the sun pops over the horizon, the fish will light up like mirrors."

Within 15 minutes of shutting down the engine, the shirt was sticking to his back. The guide knew enough about the evaporation process to understand humidity is created by moisture in the atmosphere, and that the same moisture that had his shirt clinging to his shoulders, arms and chest would bring about the daily thunderstorms that marched from land to sea every afternoon. The shirt he was wearing was made of specially-designed high-tech fibers with panels cut into the pattern to allow wind through the material and across one's body, thus creating an overall cooling effect. That's why he was shivering on the run out, but a general lack of wind completely defeated the shirt's design, and now sweat dripped down his spine. "Damn, it's not even dawn." he thought. Just enough light crept over the horizon to throw a glow into the sky and outline the distant storm clouds, which occasionally threw a bolt of lightning but were too far off for the thunder to be heard. It was still too early to see the water's surface.

"Which way will they come?" he wondered out loud, knowing full well the fish were on their northern migration.

"Relax Charlie, you'll have plenty of time. They'll likely come straight down the inside of the reef, though sometimes they like to hug the beach right at dawn to avoid the sharks."

Charlie knew enough about these fish to understand the process. At first light the school would gather in rank, the largest fish in the lead, the rest of the school staggered, sometimes only inches apart and other times in little sub groups with as much as 10 feet between the lead fish and the rest of the pack. They'd float to the surface and mill for the first half-hour, regrouping and forming a leadership of rank and file as they acclimated to the light. Usually the school would continue moving north, first at a slow pace that would take the entire group 30 minutes to cover 100-yards, then would pick up speed as they hugged the shoreline always watching for the first meal of the day.

Occasionally, a school would turn and head south, usually to feed on the same minnows that provided sustenance before dusk, as the tarpon took station for the night. It was the southward moving schools that could catch an angler off his guard and allow the lead fish to bust the boat. A slap of the tail on the water's surface would send a signal to the rest of the clan and not only put them on edge, but quite possibly deter them from feeding altogether. This little bit of knowledge was enough to keep Charlie looking over his shoulder every few minutes even though he couldn't see much farther than the bow.

"She's gonna be a nice one Charlie," he said, knowing the sun was going to come crying orange over the horizon just as it does every

June morning. "Today's the day. I can feel it."

"Today's the day," Charlie repeated several times over. "Today I get my scale."

"Visualize it Charlie. See the fish lock on. See the take. Feel the set." "This is your day. Your moment. No fish can take it from you. You're gonna rip some lips."

Charlie put his rod down and started fumbling with his shirt pocket, eventually pulling out a large brown torpedo-shaped object. He held it up to his face just under his nose and inhaled, rolling it

across his upper lip as he basked in the sweet chemically smell of rolled tobacco. He didn't have to look at the wrapper to know its origin. Charlie only smoked Monte Cristo #2's, hand-rolled Cuban cigars that he brought back 20 boxes at a time from the Bahamas.

"Today, we share the fish together," he said, then placed the cigar back into his pocket. "I feel good Miguel. Today's the day."

"The odds are with you Charlie. Lord knows you've paid your dues." They stood silent for several minutes, thinking of the last two years. Reliving all the fish. Seeing the shark and all the blood in the water, the half-bitten carcass floating on the surface and the great predator circling in the distance but in no rush to finish its meal. When it did decide to feed, it took the carcass behind the head, using its teeth to saw through the flesh in slow deliberate movements of the jaw. The end result was considerably less violent than the initial attack that sent water flying and created its own blood-stained wake. Once the shark bit the tarpon's tail off, it knew it didn't have to work for the rest of the meal. Though alive and still moving in slow, side-to-side exaggerated swings of its body, the tarpon was completely disabled, and it was just a matter of seconds before the wound emptied the body of all its vital fluids. The wounded fish's attempt at escape only increased the volume of red pumping from the wound.

Charlie reeled the line tight, grasped the side of the reel and with the same type of jerk that initially set the hook in the great fish's jaw, popped the class tippet. He then retrieved the line in silence. "Nothing you could do Charlie," he assured. "He came from under the boat. There wasn't time to break him off."

Had he seen the great hammerhead after his fish, the angler would have clamped his hand on the reel and immediately broke the line to give it a chance at survival. Harnessed to his line, the tarpon had no chance to escape. He'd been fighting it for over an hour, and the fish was already tired. Even if he did see the shark in time, the tarpon was already probably too weak to survive. The big hammerhead would run it down, dogging its every move and making it work to avoid predation so that the tarpon could never recover its strength and have a chance to put some distance between them. Though the hammerhead was born with a genetically small mouth for a shark of its magnitude, it would eventually tire the tarpon to the point it could attack from below and focus on its width, not girth.

"How big do you think it was?" Charlie asked.

"One-thirty. Could have been one-forty. She was a deep fish."

"I meant the shark."

"Twelve, maybe thirteen feet. Very beeg shark," Miguel emphasized his accent as he cranked over the motor. "Very beeg."

Two days earlier, they'd fished to the south, and although the schools were more plentiful, most were small. Of the six or seven schools that swam by the boat that morning, only one school had the fish that would break the 100-pound mark Charlie knew would rank as a new accomplishment in his fly fishing skill. He'd caught almost 20 tarpon in the two years since he started fishing with Miguel, first deliberately starting small to compensate for his fly fishing skills, and then gradually seeking larger fish as he gained experience.

They fished twice a week for three weeks in June, when the tarpon came out of the Florida Keys, following an innate route north along the eastern seaboard. Dispersing as they went, fish that were in Fort Lauderdale at dawn, could easily be dining at Palm Beach 50 miles to the north by dusk. Some fish would stay in the inlets, feeding on the larger baitfish swept out with the tide, gradually focusing on the minnow schools as they worked their way up into the rivers. The majority of the fish would continue north, until the last few migrating tarpon settled near the pogy schools along the Carolina coast.

On that day, there was an extreme low tide and the fish couldn't get over the rocks, so the school came slowly down the outside of the reef, maybe 20 in all, but not a fish under 120-pounds. When Charlie finally saw the lead fish, it was only 30 feet out and slightly to the right, and he had to adjust his right-handed cast so that he didn't catch his guide with the backcast.

The first cast fell short and to the right of the lead fish, and instead of letting it settle in hopes the fish might locate the color and make a direction change, Charlie picked it up again, made one false cast to reload the rod, and plopped it directly behind the lead tarpon's tail.

"Leave it", said the guide. "The next fish is almost as big. Let it sink a second."

Five seconds went by, and Charlie could feel his right leg starting to quake just a bit.

"Okay, strip it. Strip it slow Charlie. Don't hop it. Long, deliberate pulls. Shake the rod tip. Swim it. Swim it like a fish."

As he made the strips, he was careful to focus on the fly, making sure he didn't lose the tiny tuft of feathers when the big fish appeared behind it. Twice before he'd watched the fish, thinking he'd see a dramatic strike, but ended up losing the fly. Although the guide yelled to set the hook, the fish had never changed speed or the cadence of its tail, never gulped or charged, only turned off, and he was sure it was a denial.

"You've got to pay attention Charlie,"his guide had said. "You, me, the fishâ…We're all following the fly."

This time, the fish came into his vision as a backdrop to the traveling fly, kicking its tail rhythmically with the strips of the line, only covering twice the distance. It closed the gap rapidly, drawing to within a few feet before opening and closing its mouth and turning off. Charlie hit the fish hard, bending the rod to his side and strip-striking in unison.

There was an instant of energized motion with everything coming hard at the boat. Rod, line and fish all moved forward in one slow, deliberate movement, then reversed direction and sucked a wall of energy back to sea. The rod bounced straight, then arced again, with the line climbing off the deck in a blur, pulling tight and overflexing the rod as the fish took to the air. Charlie stood dumbfounded, looking at the reel.

MEXICO RETURNS

"Line caught on your belt buckle. Nothing you could do Charlie. It just happens that way sometimes."

But he knew there was more to it. He had to watch the line, make sure he wasn't standing on it and that every inch was stripped onto a clear section of deck. He could lead the line to the reel by holding his fingers in a loop and guiding the flow. He thumbed the cigar in his pocket unconsciously, forming small loops with his thumb and forefinger.

"Today is the day," he thought to himself.

"Charlie," the guide said in a low whisper, bringing the angler back to reality. "A hundred and fifty yards. One o'clock."

The old man lifted his head in the direction off the bow as his eyes gained their focus. In the distance, a single fin flashed black against a sheet of liquid mercury. Ten feet behind the fish, small wavelets humped the surface sending ripples in all directions.

"I see them Miguel. How Big?"

"I've only seen the lead fish. She's too far off. Maybe, maybe not."

The two watched in silence, waiting for a fish in the school to fin out or roll hard. Charlie stripped the line out of his reel testing the drag with his hand and placing the line in deliberate coils on the deck. The rod in his right hand, he found the fly with his left, pinching the hook. Two fish at the rear of the school rolled simultaneously. "How big Miguel?"

The guide shook his head up and down. "Beeg enough. Lead fish is a beast."

"This is you day Charlie. This is your moment. You'll never catch another one like your first one."

He released the hook and made a small false cast to get the hackles wet so the fly would sink quickly.

"Savor it Charlie. No fish can take it from you. Feel the rod and the line in your hands. Feel your double-haul. See the fish follow and eat."

At 100-yards, the school made a turn towards shore, but the lead fish surfaced back in line with the reef, and the rest of the school tracked back out.

"Hard strike Charlie. Feel the hook go in."

Eighty yards out, the school submerged.

Ten seconds elapsed.

Then twenty.

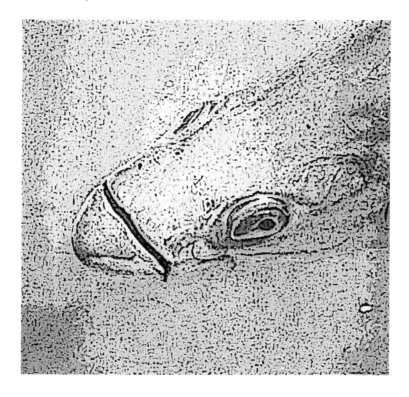

MEXICO RETURNS

Charlie could feel his grip tighten on the rod. "Where are they Miguel? I don't see them." He said the words just fast enough to emit a sense of urgency. "Relax Charlie. They're still coming down the reef. You own them. They have no idea we're here."

Another 10 seconds of silence.

"Ten thirty, forty yards. You can just see the tip of the fin from the lead fish. Get ready Charlie, this is your time."

At last the old man caught a glimpse of black slicing an inch above the surface. Not much to keep track of the school with, but enough to follow the lead fish. Hunching his profile, he brought his left foot slightly forward and released the fly.

"Keep it smooth Charlie. Use your double haul." He could feel the rod flexing with the forward and backward extensions of the line as he paid the excess off the deck. When the rod loaded, he felt the weight change through his wrist.

"Let it go Charlie. Now." The line shot forward, rolling out and depositing the fly 15 feet ahead and in the direct path of the moving fin.

"You're there. Let it sit. Let her come to you. Let her see the fly."

"Slow, long strips Charlie."

In rote fashion, he made one long pull on the line, then released it and regained his grip near the rod. He stripped again.

"She's locked on Charlie. Coming hard."

He stripped it again, straining to see the fly through the morning glare. He still hadn't found the fly when he saw a flash of silver and a small boil on the surface. Instinctively, he set the hook.

"Holy mother of god," yelled the guide. The fish was three jumps and

75-yards out by the time the words touched his ears. "She's a beeg one Charlie. One-forty, maybe one-fifty. You own her now Charlie."

The old man looked down at his reel. All the line and half the backing were already gone. He wasn't sure if he could stop the fish. "She's going too fast Miguel," he blurted, each word gaining volume. "You're going to have to start the boat."

The guide turned up the throttle on the trolling motor, and the boat lurched forward, shifting the angler's momentum, but not enough to ease the pressure he was putting on the fish. Two more times the fish cleared water, each jump drawing a whistle from the guide. After the second jump, the tarpon made a long glide along the surface, arcing towards the shore.

"You've stopped her Charlie. She's charging the beach. If we can get her into the shallows, she'll jump more, and that will take her strength. Keep the pressure on. Down and dirty."

The angler pulled hard to the side, exerting maximum pressure on the rod, and switching the tension to the opposite side as the fish changed directions. Whichever direction the fish opted to take, the angler would counter by maneuvering his rod to the opposite side to get a strong pull across the fish's body. He knew if he could bend the fish's neck just once, he could roll it over and end the fight. By applying side pressure, he could stop the fish in its tracks, and make it swim with its neck pulled back.

The guide lifted his wrist. "Eighteen minutes. You've taken a lot out of her in a short time. The runs are getting very short now."

"Yes, but I can't stop her. It's a battle of attrition. I take in ten feet and she takes back twenty."

"It only seems that way. The fish has been the same distance from the boat. When you cut that distance in half, you stand the best chance of losing her. Most fish are lost when you can see the leader. No mistakes Charlie. She wants you to make a mistake."

MEXICO RETURNS

The old man applied pressure to the reel and the fish made a hard surge with its tail, forcing him to remove his hands. Then it ran directly at the boat.

"Follow her Charlie. Get your rod tip in the water. She's going under." He was way ahead of the fish, leaning forward and stuffing the top third of the rod under the surface and gently gliding the rod to the opposite side of the boat. The fish greyhounded, leaping wildly three times in the space of ten feet.

"See how she couldn't get out of the water on the second jump? She's tired Charlie. She's still only 20 yards out. You own her now Charlie. Put the heat on her. Don't let her rest."

The old man palmed the reel again, preparing for a tail surge that didn't come. The fish was making a lot of direction changes, but he could see it was steadily losing ground to the reel. He palmed the spool again and slowly tested the flex of the rod.

The line came up as the fish rose to the surface, kicking its tail in a slow, steady cadence. The old man leaned into the rod stopping the fish, then bending its head back and rolling it upside down.

"You rolled her Charlie! You rolled her! You own her now! No mistakes!"

Twice more he rolled the great fish which eventually settled into feeble attempts to swim straight down. He stopped her in her tracks, pulling her backwards through the water column.

She came to the surface on her side.

Miguel softly grabbed the bite tippet and led the fish to his waiting hand, stuffing his fingers into her mouth and locking on the outside with his thumb. The fish shook its head, but the guide did not lose his grip. He reached for his pliers.

"Don't worry about the scale Miguel. Just set her free."

The guide removed the fly and revived the fish before watching it swim off. He looked back at the old man who was sitting on the foredeck, feet in the cockpit, the cigar already lit. He wiped the sweat off his forehead with his bandana, examined the leader for wear and handed the tippet forward.

The old man smiled, and then used the cigar to melt the leader just above the fly. He put the fly in his shirt pocket, then leaned his head back and watched the cigar smoke drift from the boat.

"You're right Miguel," the old man puffed. "Everyone is watching the fly."

Vasectomy

Cut my nuts please
Lenny

OK, after reading about Salmo and his 6 curtain-climbers running around the house I realize the time has come. i need to get clipped. 2 Kids, Im nearly mid-40's, married 10 years, house, good job.......all that bullshit.

Any horror stories I should hear about?

A few years ago, I open my stocking on Christmas morning to see...The business card from a local Urologist...So I say to the wife, "What the fuck are you thinking?"...to which she replies, "I made an appointment for you, it's next Friday"...I say, "Did you also hire four big fucking gorillas to drag me in there? And they better not live in this town, because I PROMISE you, I will put a bullet in every one of those motherfuckers in the next six months"...

She drops the issue...

Few months go by, and she's pregnant again... Fuck woman, take care of yourself...You put those pills on the sink right next to your toothbrush...See what happens when you don't brush your teeth"...

Slept downstairs for two months for that comment...

Anyway, I finally decide, "What the hell, I want to have a new car some day, so I better stop popping out these crumb snatchers", and make an appointment...And now, my friend, we come to the part of my post where I can help you...

I didn't sleep a wink the night before, because no matter how many people tried to placate my fears, I couldn't get over the thought of having a needle stabbed into my boys...I don't care what anyone says, that is going to HURT...But....And this is the big buffalo butt that MikeO so loves...But what no one tells you is that they don't stick your boys, just the bag...They pinch the bag, numb the skin and cut it...you never feel the needle...THEN when they open the incision, they put the needle into the tube (vas) that leads to your boys, something that again, you don't feel...and numb the boys out... Only then do they cut the spaghetti...While they're pulling on it you feel a weird sensation in your neck, like someone is yanking on your carotid....But it's all over and done with minimal pain and maximum humiliation...

They tape your unit to your hip bone, pack everything tight in a jock and send you walking slowly out the door (AKA the walk of shame)...You get to eat pain killers, drink brown whiskey and watch football all weekend....

On Monday, the entire package turns purple...take pictures, you'll want them so you can fuck with the whiney bitches that are next in line...By Tuesday at the latest, you're back to work...

Now, you seem like a decent guy, so I'm going to save you some embarrassment...

1. EXPECT the nurse to say, "Wow, that's like a HUGE FUCKING PENIS....Only smaller...

MEXICO RETURNS

2. When they ask you to shave the area, don't shave your entire bag...It's fucking Ghey...If you do, the nurse will make a comment like," Oh let's stick a finger in his ass and see if he gets a hard-on"...

3. Do not go home if you have children less than 10 in the house... See what happens on Monday, and picture it with your balls swelling like nectarines when one of those fuckers jumps in your lap or punches you in the balls like every male child is prone to do at least once a day...

4. Wait at least four days before having sex...and don't even think about her being on top, cause when you pop, it's going to be audible and include flames, and you're going to want a running start...

Saudi Arabia

Saudi Aribia
D. Micus

Well, brothers, I've taken a job in Saudi Arabia on the Red Sea. Fishing looks manic; downside is no alcohol or pork (both are illegal). I hope to be posting pics of me with giant yahoo before the year is out...

Dude...SA rocks!....Most of the country is this desert highlands shit, but there are some lush areas that are full of fish...If you get a chance, head to Abha, which is a resort city near the Red Sea...Primarily highlands and very verdant...

Now SA is a monarchy, which basically means men rule and women obey...Which is why the population rate is skyrocketing, well that and they found out that camel toe was more fun than camel booty, although you'll still see statues of camels all over the country, which are basically war lord shrines to their first piece of ass...Anyway, you can bark at the women and they will oblige, so get an Arab/English dictionary and become fluent in saying "You might want to get on your knees and start apologizing" and "Have you ever had a Sandy Sanchez?"...

When you get to Abha, you want to get a guide to take you to the

MEXICO RETURNS

National Park of Asir...It's a big farming area where you'll eat well...
lots of vegetables and cows (The SA women freeze dry the tongues,
then lubricate them for use as a sexual aide)...There are two rivers,
the Rub al Khali and the Najd...Now the Najd isn't much of a river,
more of a irrigation canal, but it's full of these funky carp-like fish
that eat fruit...Anywhere you see date trees along the river, you'll
find the Southern Platyfish, which looks like a goldfish you'd find
in your aquarium, but it gets to about 20 kilos, and jumps like a
monkey on acid...

There's only one fly shop in Abha, it's called Monty's....You want
to go there early in the day and ask for Syed...Tell him you want to
fish the Najd and need some date flies..The call them Foufou, which
means chocolate salty balls in Arabic...Syed has a rack of them in
the back, because they're illegal to have out in public, since they
look like the male genitalia...Get yourself a pocketful of Foufou,
and head for the river...

Now here is the Key...When heading for the Najd, you have to
pass through a town called Zeb, which is a notorious Mecca for
smugglers...You can get anything you want in Zeb...You want
the macking hash bombs that roll into sticky goo that tastes like
Nirvana and makes you immediately nap in the dirt, they got it...
You want the space cakes (there they like cookies) that let you
converse with the animals, they've got it....But if you stop be careful,
and don't wander far from your guide...

Zeb is basically a shithole of a town, but it has this HUGE arena,
and it's home to the world's largest genetic freak show...Oh, and
Arabs are the freakiest, freaks when it comes to that stuff...It's
all sexually oriented...They've got the lady with four breasts, the
beardedest clam, the chick with the monkey paw...the girl with
two glass eyes that can take them out and wink you off...You know,
freaky freak...

Anyway, if you walk into Zeb with a pocketful of Foufou, they're
going to notice you've got the golf ball lap, which is some kind of
Muslim sign of fertility...If they spot it, they won't let you out of

the place until you prove your manlyhood by splooging the freaks, which in itself is kind of a turn-0n/once in a lifetime opportunity better than nailing Siamese twin biatches in which one of them is a midget...Except...Except for the fact that it's taboo for you to take you pants off, so everything has to take place through the zipper... Now I know you're thinking, no biggie, but you've got a pocket full of foufou flies with these big ass French hooks in them, and the minute you start poking, they're going to be poking back...

Did I mention that all this will be public?...In an open air arena?... With a bunch of rich Arabs watching and betting on how long you'll last...And cause each one of them has money on it, they'll get some massive guy named Hassan with no shirt and a GIANT knife to stand behind you...And any time you slow down, they'll yell SALAMATU!!!...Which means "Stab him in the ass" in Arabic...

So your little stop for a ball of Nepalese gooey turns into this stoned and smezzed out nightmare where you're squatting over the Queen of Lippia Vulva while Hassan pokes you in the ass and the Foufou stabs you in the nuts as you do your best to maintain an erection and not laugh at the pussy farts...

Or, you could just haul along some small tarpon flies and fish the Rub al Khali for Indo-Pacific tarpon and be a stick in the mud...

Madonna

Madonna cheats on A-Rod with a Brazilain model.
JRH

How could she do this to A-Rod?

P.S. Madonna is like 75. brazilian dude is like 20. He can't pull any hot brazilian ass?

Trufh or Dare?...I've been trying to stay out of this thread cause it's a little too close to home...And for some reason I thought I'd get called out on it because some of you know me, and probably knew about the story...

Anyway...You have to know M, to understand her...She's actually extremely smart, very open and brash, and fun as hell to be around...A lot of her persona is just an act that sells music... She's a workaholic, and super picky about what she eats, drinks, etc...I only saw her drinking water or fresh squeezed juice the entire time...

I have some friends that I fish with that live on Palm Beach Island. I was around 30, so we're talking somewhere around 1990 or 91, and this friend always had a big Christmas party on Palm Beach

Island...It was right when William Kennedy Smith was on trial for raping Patricia Bowman...So I get invited to this party...Pull up in my truck, and there's maybe 20 valet parkers in front of the house, and they'd jump in your car, and park it somewhere on Palm Beach Island...Which was funny as hell watching them try to drive a stick and parallel park it between the Jags and Mercedes...

Unbelievable house on the water, two big tents with food next to the pool, DJ, big crowd...And I remember the WKS thing, because the trial was going on during the day on TV, but at the party, both sides and their legal teams were there...One tent had Bowman and her crew..the other had Kennedy Smith and his crew...It was weird as hell, and tense any time you got around those people...A-N-D... It was the same night as the debutante ball in Palm Beach, so you had all these young hotties in evening gowns blowing through...

There's maybe 500 people or so at this house....And I go to take a piss in the pool cabana bathroom, and while I'm at the urinal, someone walks in, and I look over and it's Billy Idol...sure as shit... Can't miss him with the hair and the outfit...

I'm pretty lit, so I yell over to him.... Billy! What the fuck are you doing in Palm Beach, Billy! ?...He says, "Well Madonna and I drove up from South Beach...We started talking about the Kennedy Smith thing, then he was asking about the beach and where to go body surfing...I was working on the beach as a lifeguard at that time, so was the obvious surfer/stoner/vagabond in the crowd... Then he was asking about spliff and where he could score...

Ten minutes later, we're drinking beers by the pool, and I look over and standing about 10 feet from me is Madonna...She's really easy to pick out of the crowd, cause her and Idol both have this glowing white hair...She's got these two GIANT fucking goons with her, and I could tell from the start that they didn't like me one bit...I stepped forward to introduce myself, and this one goon steps in, puts his hand on my chest and says, "You need to step back. ?... She sees this, and steps in, asks the goon if he's ghey...He says, "no ma'am, why?... ?She says, "Well then why are you feeling him up?...

MEXICO RETURNS

He starts to answer, and she just looks at him, smiles, grabs my hand and pulls me into the conversation...

She's talking to two other women, a blonde and a brunette... both smoking hot...Idol is pulled off to the side with a babe that definitely wants in....The two girls are from Australia...and while we're talking the brunette mentions that she just got back from a week of black marlin fishing...That just opens the book, and I'm rattling off fishing stories, and we're telling dirty jokes, and making fun of the Kennedy Smith group...Just having a blast...

So the brunette excuses herself to go to the bathroom, and Madonna goes with her...I go get another drink...come back...the blonde is talking with Idol and the chick he's now hooked up with...I talk with the blonde for a while...but Madonna and her friend don't show up...So I ask the blonde... Hey where's your partner in crime?...She says, "My what?...I say, "you know, your friend, the girl that was with you...She says, in a kind of tooky voice, "Why, do you like her?....So I reply, "I think she's cool as hell, and her accent just eats me alive...And that's when she got the look on her face like I'd just kicked her dog...

She says, "THAT'S MY MOTHER in this real crappy tone... And at the exact time she says it, a server carrying a giant frozen orange drink bumps into her shoulder and dumps the drink down the front of her shirt...

Idol starts laughing hysterically, and tells her to just fucking take the shirt off...But she's fuming....She goes stomping off into the house....And like a dumb ass nice guy, I follow her inside and try to help her find a sink and a dryer...I wander in the house with her for about 10 minutes, until she stops me, calls me a Cocksucking surfer asshole, and flares off...

So I shake my head, walk away and am working my way out of the house, when the goon bodyguard that put his hand on my chest tells me the girls are in the library...I go inside, and no shit, there's about 20 women sitting around a fireplace with a lit fire telling stories and dancing to the music from the DJ outside…And there's a fucking mound of beak on the table…And I look around, and I see Idol, and two other guys, and Idol now has three or four girls working him while he's dancing…And every couple of minutes he dances over and sticks his face into the pile of whiff…It was a total freak show…The entire time Madonna was trying to get Idol to pull his pants down and let the girls shove something up his butt…

The party was on a Friday night, which was fortunate because Friday and Saturday were my days off, but I had to call in vacation days for Sunday, Monday and Tuesday…It was fun as hell…We all ended up at The Breakers Hotel, and I spent most of my time with the brunette, who ended up married to a gazillionaire…Ya'all probably read about that in People Magazine…

Naples

Naples info?
Tx.

Maniac is on the road to Naples to help a buddy move.
He will have a day or two to fish, has access to a boat.
PM me w/ any hotspotting info please, or if you're open to fish he'd dig
that, too.

THX

Naples is very cool. Kind of a small town right on the beach...
Gulf has been kind of cold lately, but I guess the snook bite in
Chocko has been off the chart on the warm days...If you go south
down 41 to 951 and over onto Marco Island, right after Trapper
Custom Marine on the left is Andrew Bostick's house, but he's
usually hanging with his kids or his dad, so it's better to go a few
more streets down and the road jogs left and turns into Collier
Blvd., which is a main thoroughfare through the hotel district...
About a half mile down on the right is the Marriott Beach Resort
and Spa. And right in front of there is a nice section of rocks that
are covered in snook on the warm days...Now don't pull into their
driveway, as the hotel pays a goon squad to come out and fuck with

the people who park there but aren't staying there…I'm pretty sure the fat fucker with the flattop is a corpse fucker, which I don't get at all, as I'm usually complaining when a chick is a dead fuck, but that guy's like 6' 4" and 290, so I imagine he's squeezed the life out of a woman or two just by climbing on top of them, and now it's turned into a fetish…But in talking with Bostick, the guy is gay, which makes him a Necrophilihomo of the worst kind…

Instead, park at the 7-11 across the street…Go into the 7-11 and ask for Gurmeet, who is usually behind the cash register or fixing the Slurpee machine…Give him $10, point towards your car and say, "Beach"…

If Gurmeet isn't there, his sister Nania is usually running the register…Nania's English isn't very good, so when you hand her $10, point to the car and say "Beach", she'll think you're saying "Bitch", and usually will smile at you…Don't smile back…Cause Nania will think you're looking for a quickie in the car, and if you're older than 40 (in India culture, older men are considered sexy) she's going to show you her breasts, which though nice, have a lot of hair on the nipples, which I guess is a cultural thing, but kind of creepy in my book…Anyway, by the time you've reacted and start explaining the mistake, Nania will have grabbed a pack of Trojan Magnums and a bottle of Astroglide from the shelf and will be heading for the beer cooler, thinking you're going to want some refreshments to go with your happy ending…Even though Nania is only in her early 20s, the culture teaches the women to be open and accommodating with their sex, as the man is the ruler of the house and the woman is there to obey and meet his needs, so Nania will likely hop into the front seat of your rental, lean over the top of the seat, flip up her dress and ask you to lube her up from behind…And knowing you guys, any chance at nailing a young gun is a chance to knock a twitchy one out, so you're going to jump at it…

One thing you want to know about Nania is that she's really into birding…She's the president of the Audubon Society of Naples, and has like a gazillion birds in her house… So while you're sitting in the drivers seat so to speak, lubing her up from behind while she's

bent over the seat and leaning into the back seat, she's going to 47
see your fly boxes…Did I mention that Nania is an India word for
Curious Cat?…Well, you'll be rooting around in her box and she'll
be rooting around in your fly boxes, and when she opens one and see
the flies…Well, there's this freaky part of the culture that teaches
the women to belly dance and build and control all the muscles
in their lower torso…and when she sees those feathers, she's going
to tighten up, and you're going to be stuck and knotted up like a
pair of dogs, and Nanai has some kind of anxiety disorder where
she flies off the table and TOTALLY FREAKS OUT and runs
screaming…Only she doesn't r-e-l-a-x the muscles first…

So the next thing you know, she's clawing her way out the door,
dragging you behind her (or if you're lucky you'll be able to wrap
your legs and get a good grip) as she runs screaming down the
street…Either way, Nathan, the local Cop with the one bullet (who
also happens to be Nania's boyfriend) is likely going to spot you
or get the 911 call, in either case you're screwed…Literally…Now
Nathan may be a dumb as a shovel inbred mongoloid, but he's also
a good old boy with a BAD temper…And odds favor that by the
time he gets to the scene, Nania will have dragged you over to the
Marriott, which is where Nathan is going to have to hit you with
the stun gun to get you to relax enough for your Johnson to shrivel
enough for the two of you to part…And that's where he's going to
leave you…Unconscious…With fat ass Necriphilihomo, two more
Magnum Trojans and a bottle of Astrogilde…The guy is going to
think God brought him a smorgasbord…So in the long run, it's
probably better to just walk the beach south of the Naples Pier
cause that doesn't kill your ass too bad…

If you've got time, try the bass fishing in the Everglades Canals…
It's going off right now, as the water levels are dropping in the
marsh, forcing the fish into the canals…It's literally 100 fish days…

From Naples, head west on 75/which merges with 84 to form
Alligator Alley/Everglades Parkway, and you'll hit a buttload of
canals that are full of bass, along with boat ramps if you're hauling…
The hot fly is called the Speckled Bee, which is a popper variation

with spots on it...Farking outfishes everything else three to one...
You'll probably be able to find a bunch of production Speckled
Bee's in the fly shops in Naples, but the originator of the pattern
is Sasha Yoblanovich from Miles City, which is along 75/84 about
15 or so miles west of Naples...

When you hit Miles City, turn right on 29 and then right again at
the third dirt road (I think the second one is Jones Ave.)...At the
end of the street is the Bi-The-Wayside Tavern, which Sasha owns...
Sasha has a cork board covered with photos of her fly patterns that
she sells for $2 each...Oh, and a tip about Sasha...She's smoking
hot with long legs, dark brown hair and the sexiest eyes you've
ever seen, and she oozes sex...Oh, and she's a HUGE fan of The
Pretenders and Chrissie Hynde, so she's either dressed in leather
pants and a biker jacket or all black with a white buttondown, but
you can bet they'll be skin tight...

The Bi-The-Wayside Tavern has a big bar and a bunch of tables,
and likely will be filled with people if it's after 11 a.m....Most
of the people in there are locals, kind of hardcore, but definitely
friendly...When you go in, ask for a handful of Sasha's Speckled
Bee/Hyndes...And a word of warning; Sasha is a brunette...If
there's a skinny blonde with a giant fake rack, that's her sister Karina,
who besides working as a bartender is a hell of a fly caster in her
own rights...I've seen Karina throw an entire line with just the
top half of the rod in her hand...Anyway, Karina is a nympho, and
bi-sexual, and if you ask for a Speckled Bee/Hynde, she going to
come back with, "How'd you like to speckle my be-hind"...Don't
fall for it...It's code to the rest of the people in the club that you are
also bi-sexual, thus the name of the place BI-The Wayside Tavern...
Before you know it, you're drinking shots of Vodka from between
Karina's tits while she's rubbing up against you and dripping on
your foot...But come morning, you're going to be the one to wake
up tied to the table naked with a speckled be-hind...

But that's only if Karina is working. Sasha is proud of her flies, and
if she's working, she'll likely engage you in conversation to get a feel
for your fishing prowess...If you tie, she'll bring you into the back

MEXICO RETURNS

where the bench is and show you her Speckled Bee/Hynde…Then
tie up a handful and sell them to you for $2 each…It's all kind of
weird, mainly because of Sasha's total infatuation with everything
that is The Pretenders and Chrissie Hynde…I mean, she's always
talking in code and saying shit like, "Ay, oh, way to go," and "Gonna
use my, my, my imagination"… And she's dressed in leather and all
dark, and the tavern is dark…And you've got this snapping hot babe
in front of you that's a total sexpot and she's really into the fly scene,
so you kind of get the illusion that she's also into you, which she
definitely isn't, being married to Tiger Billy, a Seminole Indian and
the owner/operator of the Swamp Rat Airboat Rides next door…

Tiger Billy is like 6' 3" but wiry for an Indian. But a hell of a nice
guy who also owns 200 acres behind the Bi-The-Wayside Tavern,
and on that 200 acres is a series of lakes he calls the Mud Holes…
They're old gator holes that are farking full of big bass…If Tiger
Billy comes in, just ask him general fishing questions, and he'll
likely tell you all you want to know about fishing the Glades…If
you buy him a beer, he'll probably tell you about the Mud Holes…
Buy him a 12-pack, and he'll let you fish them…He's got a small
wooden boat tied off to a makeshift dock that two people can use,
so if there's two of you, one can pole and the other can cast…It is
the single best bass fishing you will ever experience in your life, and
a day you will talk about for years…

The problem with fishing the Mud Hole is that it's so good, you
don't want to leave, which means you'll be fishing until dark,
catching a bass on every second or third cast… By the time you get
back to the dock and walk the dirt road back to the Bi-The-Wayside
Tavern, it'll be packed…As long as it's not a Tuesday or a Thursday,
you'll be fine…Go in, grab your car keys, thank Sasha and Tiger
Billy and leave…Did I mention that they make you leave your keys
at the tavern as a deposit against you throwing your trash around
or wrecking the boat?…They do…Now if it's Tuesday or Thursday,
those are Two-for-one Transvestite nights, and here's where the
weirdness starts…Every one of those fucks dresses like Chrissie
Hynde, with a black wig and everything…So you walk in, and
there's a bar full (I'm talking 200 or more) of Sasha's, and it's dark

as hell, and you're going to have to pick the right one to thank for letting you pole Tiger Billy's Mud Hole and tell how much you like her speckled bee/Hynde…

Lake El Salto

fly fishing in Mazatlan?
Midstream

I am going to Mazatlan next week. Is there any fly fishing at all there?
Everything I am finding says very little about fly fishing, mostly deep
sea stuff for Marlin. Thought maybe someone here might know. I get
to smoke a bunch of Cuban Montecristos either way, but would love to
finally get to use my Scott STS 8 wt (really lays it down) and abel super
8 for something more that filler in my safe.

Dude. About an hour or so north and slightly west of Mazatlan is Lake El Salto, which is just insane when it comes to bass fishing...My biggest there was 13-2, but that was in June, when the water was down and everything was dead...As a rule, the fishing is fast and furious, but it's hot as a bull monkey's crotch...The lake is frigging giant, but you can rent a boat and a guide for about $40 American once you get there...

And getting there isn't a big deal...Rent a car at the Mazatlan Aeropuerto, as opposed to going to the Hertz dealer, which is right near the beach at Mazatlan, and directly across the street from Senor Frogs, which is just down the block from La Botana, the

Mexican version of a local strip club...The cars are cheaper at the aeropuerto because the main rental dealership is on the strip, so to speak...But more about that later...

Rent a tank, or whatever vehicle they have in stock that best resembles a tank, cause until you've driven that coastal highway, you've never understood the definition of "Bad Driver" Oh, and look up "Horn honking mother fucker too"... Anyway, if there are four of you in the vehicle, it's probably a five beer ride, so you might as well get a case of Pacifico's...The drive is beautiful, and there are all these dirt roads that turn off onto deserted coastline with waves lining up like corduroy lines of cocaine on a blue mirror, and little palaces sitting on the hill's just beautiful, and captivating, and inviting...And you have to pee...

But don't even think of pull off down one of those roads, because while it looks like an innocent vacation home on the hill, it really belongs to Carlos and Miguel and is part of their personal cartel hacienda/marijuana farm...As you get down the road and start looking for a tree to piss on, you'll notice that there really aren't any trees, just the giant nursery pots with the dark green mesh shades over them; and well, shade is shade, so you'll eventually give up looking for the tree, get out, sneak under the fence and under the shade tarps to pee, and that's when you'll realize that the nursery pots have plants in them...Pot plants...AND, since you're already pretty lit, your better judgment will be back in Mazatlan at the cerveza emporium, so you'll do what everyone always does, you'll pull six or seven plants and carry them back to the car, where Carlos and Miguel will be waiting, Stainless Colt Python 357's stuck in their belts, as they lean into the passenger side of the vehicle and ask your wife if she's looking for a date...As you trip over the fence dragging two handfuls of hemp stalk across the ground...

Here's where I can help you out...If you get into trouble along the west coast of Mexico, you want to use my name...Tell them you are a friend of Miguel Patricio...They'll look confused at first... That's because they can't imagine why such pasty-legged geek with a turned up collar would throw my name out there, when you obviously don't ever venture over to the dark side...But with any luck, they'll see the rod tubes and put it together...From there, they're going to put hoods over your head, take you down the beach on the back of ATV's and over to the Federale HQ, where you will give them $60 each to be free and on your way...So in other words, DON'T STOP TO PEE!!!

Either way, once you get to El Salto there are a couple of fishing lodges you can use like Angler's Inn, which rocks, particularly the food and the fact that every time you walk in the front door whether it's coming back from fishing or a nap, there is someone waiting with a tray of margarita's...But if you pass Angler's Inn, follow the road down the mountain and into the valley and right up to the lake, you'll see a bunch of Mesquite trees and five or six boats tied up next to them, along with the back seat of a Buick station wagon and a cooler full of ice water...That is Javier's Place...He'll rent you the boats... The fishing is unreal whether you throw poppers or anything that looks like a baitfish...If you push up near the dam, watch for the cattle that come down the mountain to drink... Those fuckers can swim like an otter, but they can't climb into a boat worth a fuck...And don't use my name at the lake, cause I'd like to fucking fish there again...

So after your 60 bass a person with a 4 pound average and six to 15 over 8 pounds day, you're going to be pretty jazzed, and have to pick up another case of Pacifico's for the ride back; and when you get to Mazatlan, you're going to remember that I said NOT to go to the downtown rental because it's near the strip club, at which point you'll pull out your printout of this thread, head to the strip, park and ask the first Mexican you see where you can find La Botana... So let me preface your trip with the knowledge that Mexico is a bit religious, and family oriented, and not really into that decadence scene that America seems to thrive on...That being said, Mexico is also poor as parched Earth, and there are people who will do anything for a dollar...And you smendricks have mucho dinero...

When you enter La Botana, it's very dark and loud, like most strip clubs...But unlike most strip clubs, the bar will have lots of women

sitting at it...They are locals looking to pick up a rich sponsor...
That is not you...Don't piss those girls off, or they will put their
hands down your pants and grab your dick, which you will think
is an attempt to turn you on, because you didn't notice they first
rubbed jabenero jelly on them...But you'll know that pretty much
right away...If you don't get the fire dick treatment, just order a
beer sit down and shut the fuck up, watch the women dancing and
enjoy the day...If you get loud and obnoxious, they'll think you're
drunk, and will keep asking you to go to one of the side rooms for
$50...And since there's a major language barrier, you'll think it's for
a quickie...Did I mention that ALL the women in La Botana are
smoking hot?...With just snapping butts?...Well they are...And
none of them are prostitutes...The side room is for the contest...
You give them $50, and there's a woman lying on the floor with a
box over her face that has a toilet seat on it...You're expected to
dump on her face in 10 seconds...If you do, you get $500...They
take the box off and let you see she's beautiful; about 22, smoking
hot...So then the pressure is on for you to dump on her face or
sacrifice the $50 to being a dumbass gringo...

There are three ways to look at this...One; you just wasted $50,
which isn't a bad idea since you've learned a lesson about traveling
abroad and had a great day on the water... Two; you can get an
attitude, squat over the hottie and pull your pants down...And
when you lay your ass over her face, she's going to stick an ice cube
in your taint, and you're going to jump out of your pants and piss
all over the front of them in one motion, so you'll have to spend
the rest of the evening walking funny in piss stained pants...In
which case, EVERYONE in town will know you wanted to shit on
some pretty girl's face...Or... You can smile, straddle the girl, and
when the guy goes to count out the 10 seconds, you can pull your
pants down, squat and dump all in one motion, assuring she gets
mustard faced...This helps if you already have the Mexican squirts
beforehand...Then fucking run, If you live, you'll have a great story
to tell every Thanksgiving...

Maui

Anyone no about maui
flyman241

Im heading to maui for spring break and want to know if anyone has any info they would be willin to give up on fly fishin from the beach? Ive been searchin the web and came up with some pretty crappy results. Help if you can.

The thing you want to remember about Maui is that it is a volcanic island, which basically means the beaches are either rocky as a moonscape or the surf is huge enough for a wave to wash high up the dune, and suck you and your family right off the farkin' beach…Most of the big surf is on the north shore of the island….Where you want to go is on the southeastern side….Take Hwy 31 and it's just past Hana…Oh, and don't stop for a Shaved Ice at the stand in Hana…That's Dixon's place, and it's locals only, which means if you stop, some Moke is going to be wearing your clothes and sporting your girlfriend on his arm for the nightly crank AKA "Ice"bake…Just stay on the road and try not to stare like a tourist…

Check out the Seven Pools near Oheo Gulch…It's part of a river system that flows out of the mountains all the way down to the sea...Bunch of sweet ass waterfalls there...So if you bring your own wahine along, the scenery will pretty much assure you get to snap off a water chunk, which in itself if pretty funny, since there are only couples around and everyone is in some phase of entry or exit, yet everyone is trying to look like they're just hanging out in the water....I mean, you know the girl next to you isn't just sitting on her boyfriend's lap, but everyone just kind of plays along...So try not to stare and ruin it for everyone...

You don't hear much about how good the bass fishing is on Maui, although ESPN has covered it a bunch, but there are some really nice fish there, and some exotics as well, including butterfly peacocks and tucanare...If you take the Waimoku Falls Trail up about a half mile, you hit the falls sexfest, then another half mile or so you start hitting the pools...They call them the Seven Sisters after the Kaaiupa family, which had seven girls and one boy, who turned out to be a turd burglar...Go figure...Anyway, the sisters would bathe in the pools every evening, and the kings would come down from the mountain and get tightened up...so there's a bunch of royal splooge layers on the bottom of the pools...

Did I mention that this is all on the side of a giant farkin' mountain? Oh, and it's also where they grow the puna buds...So watch for pot fields...And if you run into one, don't pick anything...even your fucking nose...These guys already don't like houlies, and they're either the skinny, wiry psycho Asian or the giant fat moke, both of which would love to snap your rod over their knee and then stab the jagged edge through your throat...So just STAY ON THE TRAIL...

There's actually more than seven pools, it's more like 27 pools, and you'll find fish in most of them...Lots of bass...lots of butterfly peacocks, tucanare, Mayan cichlids, bluegill, etc....Most of the peacocks are under five pounds, but the tucanare get to 10 pounds or more...Remember that they are fish eaters, so anything that looks like a baitfish works, including Clousers...Anything that looks like a worm or insect will only catch the bass, bluegill and cichlids…This is all in the Haleakala National Preserve, so you can't kill anything…The Hawaiians believe that fish are gifts from the Gods and to be revered, so when you catch one, say Nani, which means thank you…And look up at the sky…Catch a bunch of fish, thank the Gods, have a great time, and get out of there…But ALWAYS thank the gods after you catch a fish…And be sure to say it correctly….Nah-Nee….Not Nah—Nie, which means "Piece of Shit"…If the locals overhearing you say Nah-Nie, they'll take you for another asshole exploiter, in which case, they'll likely tackle your ass into the pond, rub pond muck on you and send you down the mountain…They'll be saying, "maaopu e' anoi"and laughing as they push you downhill covered in the "itch mud" so by the time that shit dries on you, you'll be scratching like a mofo covered in grey dough….

Couple of things here… First off, maaopu e' anoi means cum face… Second, the mud itches because it has parasites in it…They're little bot worms and if you don't get that mud off you in 20 minutes, some of those bot worms will bore into your skin…And grow…So a week later, when you're back home you look at your arm and see what looks like a mole trail under your skin…That's a bot worm dude, and it's eating its way towards a major artery, where it will eventually end up in your heart, lungs or liver…None of which is good…Fortunately, your doctor can prescribe some pills that will kill it off in a couple of days…The downside of which is that you piss a dark green the entire time, and it kind of freaks you out…

Probably the best thing to do if you get muck faced is to get back in your car and stop at Dixon's shaved ice stand on the way back… Dixon has long blonde hair and talks in kind of a pig latin, so he's hard to understand but he'll be easy to pick out, because besides you, he's the only houlie in the area…Don't try to be suave or cool…Fucking run to him in a panic…tell him what happened and that Mexico from Sunset Beach told you to look him up…He may ask you to describe me, so just say, "Big guy with a tattoo of a surfboard with the word "Mom" on his chest…Dixon will take you out back for a Poi and Vinegar bath, which kills the bot worm and also makes you smell like a sour turd for about a week…Oh, and one last thing....Dixon will likely light up the biggest, fattest joint you've ever seen, and hand it to you...Don't even think of not taking a hit...Dixon will kick you out and the second you're out the door he'll yell...."No I won't sell you my land to build a condo," and the locals will think you're trying to buy up the island and force them out, in which case, you'll get a free ride out into the pineapple fields...Just take the joint...Rest assured, it's the puna bud, and you are going to take one hit, that shit is going to expand, and you are going to cough fire and smoke through seared lungs, and long before you stop hacking, you will be soooooo fucking stoned, your eyes will close into slits, in which case, if you have dark hair, you just might pass for a local...Take the bath, get $20 worth of shaved ice to soothe your throat and the munchies, and get someone to drive you home, cause I can assure you that you will no longer have voluntary muscle control, so driving yourself is out of the question unless you like flying off cliffs in a rented GEO Metro...And when you get home, change your pants before you pass out, cause you shit your pants on the way back to the hotel without realizing it... Yes, the puna buds are that strong...

Now when you wake up, you will still smell like a sour turd, and no amount of showering will get that off...Everywhere you go, people will stare and point at you and tell you how much you reek...The up side of this is that you are in Hawaii, where the inbreeding has taken place for hundreds of generations...and most of the women are in some way related to the seven sisters...and the smell of the splooge mud antidote...Well, it kind of turns them on...So you have that going for you...

Mexico's Book

For those of you that know me, you know I break the stress by writing... I've been working on a book, set back in the mid 80s about a year in the life of three people here in Floridia...One of the characters is the mate on a charter boat, who likes to fly fish and surf...In a previous chapter, he caught a marlin over 1,000 pounds in the Bahamas, and all the locals came to the dock to touch him, because they believe luck rubs off...Here's one of the chapters that involve fly fishing to a degree...Some Friday nosepicking fodder for you smendricks...

Night Moves

"You bitch," spat Calvin through rage clenched teeth. "You better come through for me this time, or I'm trading you in. This is your last fucking chance!"

The motor fired; willed to start by the intimidating character assault. By now, it was well after dark. The lights of the Nuclear Power Plant glowed ominously to the south, illuminating the surrounding miles of unspoiled mangrove shoreline in a doomsday aura.

Calvin thumbed the throttle, increasing the flow of gas and commanding the engine to react with a high pitch roar as the pistons responded with a burst to life. Confident that the engine was now warm but still hesitant to relax on the throttle, he slid the choke back a notch and flipped the shifter into gear, lurching the boat ahead on fuel-forced momentum.

The craft slid foreword now, barely up on a plane and sending a green phosphorescent glow to either side as the bow sliced the diatomaceous water. Gradually, he increased the speed, climbing to a skipping plane over the perilously shallow eelgrass, the shoreline blanketed by miles of mangroves along this desolate, undeveloped stretch of the island. Turning the corner of Blind Creek, a heron stalking the sandbars after dark screamed its protests over the steady hum of the motor, taking to flight off the port bow. Plenty of startled birds have lost their lives by either flying ahead of, or directly into an oncoming motorboat, often injuring the occupants as well. But this was not the case, as the towering bird redirected its flight pattern at the last second, dispatching phantom air currents across Calvin's shoulders and neck.

"Damn, that was close," he thought. "What else could go wrong tonight? I already broke my best rod and had the engine puke out. Now all I need is to be skewered by a kamikaze heron. Shit, I should have just stayed home."

The thoughts were still fresh, when the outline of a building or some type of elongated structure appeared directly in his path. Were there even a hint of a moon, the shape of a Cigarette boat tucked against the shoreline would have been discernible from a great distance. The fact that the boat was painted black and didn't have any running lights made it even harder to see. But on this unlit evening, it wasn't until Calvin approached within 50 feet of the craft that he noticed its presence, backing off hard on the throttle and swerving to open water to avoid a collision. As it was, he missed a near fatal smashup by only a few feet, though not completely as the boat's anchor line first tangled, then grabbed tight to the propeller, sending the surprised fisherman headfirst into the dashboard and silencing the motor for the second time that evening.

Calvin was stumped when the motor initially quit, checking the gas lines and fuel filter, and finally the spark plugs, before becoming completely annoyed with the ambiguousness of mechanics. After 35 minutes of futile troubleshooting, the sun had begun to set, and Calvin started to wonder if he was going to spend the night anchored upwind of the mosquito population that hummed aloud like a distant airfield in their bloodletting search of the mangrove shoreline. To make matters worse, he crushed the tip of his best fly rod, not remembering that he'd looped it across the floor to keep the reel from scratching against the gunwale, stepping down on the graphite while searching in vain for the emergency flare kit. His predicament would have been minor if the VHF radio was aboard, but in his haste to get on the water, the unit was left on the kitchen table. Now without the flare kit or radio, he knew he was stuck on the river until dawn.

Thoroughly pissed off and resigned to solve the mystery and spend the evening in waterbed-supported slumber, Calvin started from scratch, first checking the electrical system and then the fuel lines. He was about to give up and settle in for a night on the seaweed-encrusted deck, when the engine sputtered to life with little clue to its previous denials.

Ten minutes later, Calvin Squeezed his nose lightly, not sure whether it was broken, but certain the numbness spreading around the eyes and palate were a good indication he'd hit the windshield hard. A warm trickle ran across his fingers, crawling down the arm in webbed streams. Shaking off the impact, he peeled off his T-shirt, wound the cloth into a ball and placed it under his nose to stem the blood flow. Tilting the engine up, he stepped to the back of the back of the boat to inspect the damage.

Sure enough, the anchor line was sucked into the propeller, knotting the engine in a pressure wound mess. Scanning the area Calvin was surprised to find no one around, especially with such a valuable piece of machinery anchored in the middle of nowhere. He stood on the console for a better look at the neighboring craft, noticing for the first time the green outline of dash lights. Hair climbed straight up the nape of his neck. Someone was here not long ago. Suddenly,

Calvin grew suspicious as to the underlying motive behind the abandoned boat. No one leaves a $200,000 boat in the middle of nowhere. If his accusations were correct, someone would show up soon, and for the first time this evening, another person was not what he wanted to see.

Panicked thoughts began to swim through Calvin's head as he envisioned the possible ramifications of his predicament. Several scenarios played on his brain, all with the same outcome. Immediately, he realized one thing was as plain as the mashed nose on his face: If he didn't get out of here soon, a bloody nose and broken fly rod were going to be the least of his worries. As he frantically moved to untangle the rope from the prop, he heard the distinct sound of a shell being pumped into the cylinder of a shotgun.

"Better stay right where you are sonny," came the voice with a deep southern drawl. "I'd rather not use this if I don't have to, but it wouldn't be the first time if I did."

Freezing in mid-step, Calvin scanned the shoreline for the source of the command, finally settling on an opening in the mangroves to the left of the big boat. He moved slowly, turning to face the voice as he raised his hands in the air.

"Easy mister. I don't mean any harm," he said. "I didn't see your boat until the last minute. I'll pay for any damages I've done."

"It's not damages I'm concerned with," said the voice. "Now climb on out of that boat, and make your way to shore."

"Yes sir," he replied, a hint of hesitation in his voice. "Anything you say."

Stepping softly into the lukewarm water, Calvin shuffled his feet as he walked to shore to avoid stepping on any stingrays that might be bedding in the soft mud. This area was well known for the huge river rays that scavenged the shallows, and he'd once seen firsthand the carnage produced by their spiked tails when accidentally stepped on by a human. A wader standing next to him forgot to shuffle his feet and tromped down hard upon one of these normally docile fish. The whip-like tail thrashed, midway up the tail a sheathed, bone-encased seven inch spike, the force driving the barbed blade through the startled angler's leather wading boots, securing it well into the calf. The damage to the muscle was minor compared to the pain-inducing, bacteria-laden venom that lined the surrounding membrane. Before he reached shore, the angler's foot had swollen to the size of a softball, and the calf wasn't far behind, pain impulses rushing steadily up into the hip and thigh. Calvin knew the big man as a tough old salt, but you'd have never have known it the way he cried all the way to the hospital.

That stingray couldn't have been 10 inches across, and he'd seen a dozen or more over three feet in diameter when fishing earlier. As he moved past the speed boat, the odor of freshly harvested marijuana broke through his blood-caked nostrils.

"Shit," he thought. "Smugglers. I fucking knew it."

The myriad of inlets, canals, and mangrove backwaters that dot the eastern coastline offer hundreds of entrance and escape routes, and even after heavy pressure from the government, Stuart was still one of the top areas in the country to import illegal drugs, the smugglers making the run from the Bahamas or a from a larger mother ship that off-loaded the product into the speedboats 20 or so miles offshore. With the Bahamas only a short boat ride away, smugglers stood little chance of being detected running at night in low-profile boats that can easily outdistance any speed boat owned by the local law enforcement. As a rule, the traffickers hire commercial fishermen to operate the boats, seizing upon their vast knowledge of local waters and a lifetime of nocturnal navigation. Rarely are the boats detected, much less caught. But this person was taking no chances with the angler who stumbled upon their operation as they started to off-load their illegal cache.

"Put your hands behind your head and step up on the bank. And don't do anything foolish."

"Really mister, I didn't mean to catch your anchor line, and I won't tell anyone …"

"Tell them what?" interrupted a voice from the other side of the mangrove opening where Calvin now stood.

"Tell them that there's a boat full of drugs anchored in Blind Creek. Of course you won't. You won't tell anyone shit. Cause if you do, I guarantee we'll put a bullet in you within the next six months." Staring at the ground, Calvin tried to talk his way out of the predicament.

"Listen," he said. "I'm not going to tell anyone. Help me get my boat started, and I'll go on my merry way."

"I don't think so," answered the voice with the shotgun. "You're not going anywhere until we're safely away from this place and we're sure you can't cause us any harm. Do as we say, and you'll keep your life. Otherwise, it'll be a long time before anyone finds your body stuffed back in the mangroves."

Calvin knew these men meant business. Smuggling was a federal rap, with mandatory jail time, and though tough, these men were way too old to survive a long stint in the big house. They'd go out shooting before they'd let the law take them into custody.

"Listen," he said, "I'm not going to look up so I won't know who you are or what you look like. I'll even help you unload the bales if you want, just please let me go when you're done."

"Why that's mighty nice of you, son," said a third voice, this one from behind the boat and off to the left. "You look like a strong lad, I think we'll take you up on that offer."

For over an hour, Calvin and the three men hauled the 80-pound rectangles to shore, placing them in the back of a horse trailer that had pulled down the dirt road that ran the shoreline, only stopping for brief periods to reapply bug spray washed off areas now soaked in sweat. The darkness hid the faces of the smugglers, masking their anonymity as well as his own. After every trip to shore, Calvin expected to draw his last breath in the brackish brown waters of Blind Creek. Several times he thought about running, abandoning the idea each time as too risky, since any attempted departure would surely bring a speedy round of buckshot.

Stacked to the ceiling, 50 bales barely fit into the tandem horse trailer, even when compressed and wrapped in plastic and burlap to maintain freshness and increase storage capacity. At 80 pounds per bale, Calvin figured he was looking at roughly $800,000, given the average price of sensimillia.

By now, his nose had stopped bleeding and had settled into an annoyingly steady throb of pain. He was fairly sure it was broken, since he was having trouble breathing through one nostril and the eye above it was almost swelled shut. The sloping appendage leaned a bit to the right, although he wouldn't dare try touching it now that the numbness had dissipated.

Closing the gate of the drug trailer, the two helpers climbed into their pickup, after a quiet conversation with the man holding the gun. With a roar of rubber on loose gravel, the pair disappeared into the night, leaving Calvin and the boat captain alone in the blackness. "This is it," thought Calvin. "I'm going to die in the middle of a fucking swamp, and someone's going to have to tell my mother the land crabs ate me. Fucking great."

"You did real good, son," said the voice, now enshrouded in darkness. "Now let's start walking back to the boats."

Under the circumstances, any of a million thoughts should have been racing through Calvin's head, but all he could envision was the look on his mother's face when the state trooper told her he was crab food. Circling to the stern of the big boat, he struggled to erase the image of his tormented mother as he waited for the fatal roar of the discharged shell. Instead, he heard several loud splashes and the shocked wail of the sinister smuggler.

Calvin knew immediately that the man had stepped on a stingray, and a big one at that, since the water erupted in a teeming explosion as man and fish sought sanctuary in opposite directions. Through the darkness Calvin noticed the man on all fours, understanding instantly that the second splash came from the gun. Seizing the opportunity, Calvin drew a deep breath and disappeared under the tepid water.

Turbidity continuously muddied the Indian River, clouding the water with a brown pall of organic detritus that completely obscured visibility, even on a calm day. At night, vision was nil. Consumed in the blackness of his escape, Calvin was amazed at how far he had traveled on that one breath. His depth was detected along the way by the increased pressure on his pain-riddled face. He stroked hard, slicing silently through jellyfish-enmeshed seagrass, hoping the glowing bioluminescence of diatoms in the water now running over his body wouldn't reveal his whereabouts before he struck the deeper channel at the mouth of the creek.

The water pressure baring down on his sinus cavity bored numbed transmissions into his brain. His face throbbed and heavy pressure squeezed his sinuses. Again, he drew a large breath, descending slowly into the muddy water, heart racing ahead through the darkness. Further he swam, until he felt a burning in his oxygen deprived lungs. He emerged with a hushed burst of carbon dioxide, sucking hard on the stagnant October air. Behind, the smuggler still searched the water for his weapon, all the while spitting threats of bodily harm into the night.

True to interpretation, a stingray nearly four feet in diameter had found its mark above the knee of its vanquished tormentor, driving the foot-long barb well through his skin until impacting bone and breaking off at the base. The pain running into the injured man's hip was now unbearable, coming in waves of increasing white-hot intensity. On the edge of unconsciousness, he searched the water for his shotgun as he scanned the area for the long-haired kid. Calvin could hear the man breathing hard in the distant night. Every now and then, he'd follow a particularly labored breath with a wail of pain. Diving several more times, he eventually emerged next to the post marking the narrowest point of the channel. Clinging to the oil-soaked wood, he gathered his wits. The terrain was familiar, and he surmised that the boats lay about 100 yards to the northeast of his present position.

He was surprised that the smuggler had stepped on the ray, since an experienced fisherman would know to drag his feet in these waters, but Calvin had learned enough about misguided luck in Bimini to start asking questions now. Besides, he wasn't quite out of the woods yet. A scream of pain penetrated the darkness, followed by the sound of weight landing on the deck of the big boat.

"Shit," he thought. "He must have found the gun."

Ducking down until only the upper half of his face showed, Calvin wondered how perceptive the smuggler was to his flight after being struck by the ray. Anyone paying attention would have been able to catch a glimpse of disturbed water every time he came up for a breath, not to mention the glowing green trail he left going through the grass. Just to be sure he couldn't be tracked, Calvin sucked in a warm breath and began swimming across the open water of the channel.

Under water everything looked exactly the same...black! Having to use his hands for propulsion, anything in his path would be met head on. At any time he could swim into another channel marker or a sandbar, or even a sleeping fish like the giant tarpon that lurked up river during the late summer and early fall. Come to think of it, the majority of sharks in the river tended to congregate in these deep channels. Bull sharks. Eight footers with the girth of a pipeline and more testosterone than any animal on the planet. They'd bite first, then figure out what they're trying to eat. A shark that size could easily bite a leg off at the hip.

"Swimming at night is spooky enough without being in fear for your life," thought Calvin. "This is a lot like the feeling I get when I'm asleep and I dream that I'm falling, with no focus on what's ahead, waking in that split second before impact."

Halfway across the channel, he became disoriented and began to panic, until spotting the lights of a house on the western shoreline. Gulping another breath, he descended once again into the salty night, moving ahead with strong kicks and sweeping strokes. Nearly a decade of morning workouts at the beach had perfected his technique and formed the long striated muscles that now clawed through the water with little effort.

Rising for another breath, Calvin heard the smuggler curse and then the banging of metal against metal. Funny how sound travels in the night, he thought. Distance became obscured as the voice vibrated off his face as though right next to him. Submerging, he moved ahead, until the roar of the engine froze his body in mid-stroke. Sound travels great distances under water, the distorted inflections confusing the direction from which they come. Like the shell being pumped into the chamber of the shotgun earlier, Calvin knew the sound of the engine's roar. Submersed at night, the threatening wail of the stainless steel props became magnified.

Clearing the surface to his shoulders, Calvin strained to determine the movements of the boat. Still running without lights, the muffled engines became the only source of detection for Calvin as he wondered if the smuggler was following his bioluminescent trail. The boat putted slowly through the flats until reaching the channel, where the overpowered engines jumped to life.

In a flash of black gelcoat, the speeding boat passed within 10 feet of the terror stricken swimmer, blinding him for a brief moment with prop wash, then following it up with a slapping wake. Had he been a few feet closer to the edge of the channel, Calvin knew he would have been hamburger.

"Damn, he said as the sounds of the boat grew distant. "I guess they didn't rub off all my luck."

MEXICO RETURNS

St. Lucia

South Carribean opportunities early August?
Snapdad

Gonna somehow find myself in St. Lucia (Aug. 5th), St. Johns (6th) and then Philipsburg on the 7th of August. Can't really bring any gear as it's not really a fishing trip at all, but I want to fish. Anyone have any advice on perhaps places to go, rentals, or anything along that nature? It'd be much appreciated. I'd like to spend a day casting to something somewhere

Okay, let's break this down…St Lucia is rocking sweet, except for the fact that is was settled by the French, who besides being known for fighting with their feet and fucking with their face, they also have the most absurd (probably a French word as well) language in the world, and every farking town has a name you cannot pronounce…Anywhere along the coast the water is breathtakingly beautiful, because it comes out of 6,000 feet a half mile from land, so you get visibility like nowhere else in the world with a population of over 10,000….That all being said, there are some fish you can cast to on the north end of the island just east of Beausejour Stadium…Epouge Bay has some nice rocky shoreline habitat that draws a lot of turbot, which is a French word for butt ugly triggerfish…But, they eat flies…And they fight pretty well… Most of the turbot are four to 10 pounds, and are sight casted using any shrimp or baitfish pattern (they're pretty dumb)…

The road to Epouge Bay is called Baiseur De Moutons and it forks just before you get to Epouge Bay…Take the fork going north… It dead ends about 150 yards from the beach in a little stretch of sand…Grab your gear, and hike in…Just start working your way north along the beach, and you'll catch plenty of turbot….And whatever you do, don't take the south road on the fork…That goes to Baiseur De Moutons estate, which is this grandeur castle looking compound with high walls and Mediterranean style buildings…It's actually a swingers club…Well, more like a slave club…Men pay to have sex with females who are held captive there…Oh, and I use the term females loosely…Ewes is probably a better word, thus the name of the road (Baiseur De Moutons) which loosely translates to "Sheep Fuckers"…

Anyway, these guys take their sex life seriously, and once you drive inside the compound, you are going to be expected to put up or put out…and you know the old saying, "you can fuck a million beautiful women, but fuck one sheep or suck one"…Well, you know…
Oh, and part of the first time ritual is that that sheer your hair afterwards…So everyone on the island knows you're a member of the discreet French sect…So, you'll have to endure an endless litany of comments like….."Your hair doesn't look so baaaaaaaaaaaadddd….

Now to St. John…Most of the island is national park, with breathtaking views of mountains and the sea…beautiful beaches… and Goot Sand…No one ever talks about the Goot Sand, but if you get it on you, you will itch like a motherfucker for about five days…And I mean to the point that you can't sleep, eat or piss, cause you're an itching motherfucker….Anyway, the goot Sand is only in Grootpan Bay, which is a good thing…The bad thing is Grootpan Bay is right next to Keddel Bay and on the end of Mandel Estate Road, which is where Howie Mandel has his big chateau…The Goot Sand lies under the normal sand, so it's kind of hard to detect, and you don't start itching until you get out of the water and dry off, so the effects are neither obvious or immediate until later… Now Kiddel Bay has some pretty decent bonefish action, mostly

1-4 pounders, but a good number of fish you can cast at…Small schools and pairs running the beach mostly, but some good tailing stuff at dawn…Ghost crab patterns and tan Crazy Charlies work wonders on them…

As you wade north along Kiddel Bay, it abuts Grootpan Bay, so be careful you don't get overzealous and wander into Grootpan, which is easy because it has a ton of fish, and it's for a reason… The reason Goot Sand itches is because of a parasite called a boella worm, which lays eggs in your skin, which hatch after about an hour…The boella juveniles then spin, which separates the different layers in your skin, causing irritation…Over time, (like two or three days) they die, and unfortunately, their decaying bodies tend to bloat, so end up with small red pustules where the worms are… And dude,,,,There will be hundreds of worms under your skin, so by the fourth or fifth day, your feet and legs will be covered in red pustules, which besides waiting to pop and ooze are just the Mack Daddy of chick magnets…And don't even think about wearing shoes to cover them up, cause that will make them pop, and when they do, you won't believe the amount of fluid that comes out of that tiny pustule…And it stinks…Like sulphur…The locals have a name for the people who try to cover it up by wearing shoes, which is merde dans votre culott, and you'll hear people saying it and pointing to you on a regular basis…And your shoes will not only be squishing when you walk, but you'll have to throw them away afterwards because, dude, you're not that fucking tough that you can deal with the smell…

Now I don't know anything about Philipsburg, but with your hair shorn to a nub and the merde dans votre culotte, I'll bet you'll be a real popular guy…My suggestion would be to stay indoors…

Of course, you could always blow the dust off your wallet and hire a local guide at any of those places and avoid the typical tourist issues…

Belizean Honeymoon

So seriously... need some help
Woolybug25

I know this is bad timing considering the "Does anyone know a good guide in Belize" noob bashing incident, but fuck it, I could use some advice.

As you know Wooly, Timing IS EVERYTHING in life... With me coming back to this board, the timing seems right for some advice from the world tour...First off, asking your wife if she can put together a threesome with one of her hottie friends as a wedding present and sign of her commitment to you will piss off her big fucking goon brother when she runs crying to him and dimes you out...And it's not like that fucker likes you anyway...Better to line up a prostitute and slip a little GHB in her champagne back at the....Ah, shit, I'm getting off track...

Um, Belize...
For those of you that don't know, I am getting married this summer.

Ah-HA!...Ask for the clear jar to put your balls in...On occasion, it's nice to look at the mantle and see they're still around...

BELIZEAN HONEYMOON

She wants to go on a honeymoon somewhere warm with nice beaches,

This means she wants to go somewhere the two of you can spend the day in a lounge chair holding hands while the buff drink server leans his Johnson into the side of her face as he leans across her to hand you a frozen queer drink...P.S....There will be lots of strolls in the sand, going over lists of baby names, checking color swaths for the bathroom when you get home and quiet, expensive, romantic dinners where you'll get busted for hawking the girl sitting alone at the bar in a sun dress that you can see right through...

I want to go somewhere warm with bonefish flats.

You have no say in where you get to go...Best strategy...pay some kid to walk up while you're spooning on the lounger and tell you that there's been a terrible accident on the other side of the island and they need anyone who can espeake English to help translate for the victims...It should only take three or five hours...

Can we have both without me leaving my honeymoon divorced? I hope so. Here is what I am looking to do:

Yes, as long as you're okay with a little deceit and trickery...and she's drugged unconscious for 24 hours (remember, you can always blame it on the water), particularly if she's got a sore butt because you decided, "Hey, what the hell, she's not going to know anyway"...

1) My first choice is Belize, just because I know what it offers and the old lady likes it, but I would be open to other tropical locations (ie Los Roques, Bahamas, etc... no Mexico or keys).

Belize is good because you can walk into any pharmacia and ask for a non-barbituate hypnotic, knowing it will not show up in the autopsy should you slip a little too much in her drink...Also, Los Roques is an old South American term for "The place where the wind never stops and happiness can be found in watching the tourists stick a fly in their ear on the backcast"...And as for the Bahamas...Well, if I want the eat until you're tired, sleep until

MEXICO RETURNS

you're hungry program, I'll just walk down to the local fire station…

I am guessing that Belize is the easiest/cheapest, but I am just assuming.

Not only that, but you'll get to eat cow tongue, chicken feet soupa and plantains…

2) Close flats – I want to get a guide for at least one day, but I need close fishing too.

I totally agree here. Once you get her on the comatose routine, you can basically keep her in a stupor, which will allow you to say,"Let me get us another drink,"while you wander off, fish for four hours, and then come back and hand her a drink, and she'll think you've only been gone for 15 minutes because that is the amount of time she will be conscious during that time period…

Oh, and keep in mind…When she's in a stupor…It's open game on the pooper…

The fiance likes to fish, but she would rather read a book on the beach.

Find out what books she wants to bring, download them onto your IPOD, stick the ear buds in when she's K'O ed…and she'll be telling you how much she enjoyed those books when you get back home….

So when she is still sleeping, getting a massage or recovering from post honeymoon mind blowing sexy time (all 15 seconds of it), I can sneak off and fish on my own.

Shoot dude, you can sneak off any time you want, leaving her naked on the bed, ass in the air, with a note beside her asking the maid to turn on the sun lamp and baste her every 30 minutes….Oh, and don't forget to leave a video camera running on the dresser with a towel over it, so you can see if the maid has any bisexual tendencies and the potential for a threesome….

3) Honeymoon stuff – After all, it is my honeymoon, not a fishing trip.

74

BELIZEAN HONEYMOON

I prefer to call it a journey into celibacy, but to each his own...

*With Belize, I know that there are Mayan ruins, snorkeling, etc. I don't want to go somewhere that doesn't have this kind of cool stuff. Um...See #3....*It being a Honeymoon, and you being heterosexual, you day will likely go something like this...

Wake up...tap my lovely on the shoulder...hear from her that my breath smells like a buffalo fart...get denied a Dirty Sanchez... stagger into the bathroom to take a piss...put some GHB on her toothbrush...and in the bottle of water next to the sink...jump back in bed...tap my lovely on the shoulder again...mention that her breath, while hinting of roses, does have a scent of meat to it.... Ask if she had meat for dinner last night...watch while she gets up, brushes her teeth, drinks some water, then give her some meat for breakfast too...Look at your watch...figure you have about 21 hours before she'll wake back up...pose her for the maid...grab your rod...it's Wollybug time!!!

Here is the dilemma... we are paying for this thing on our own, so I need to cut costs as much as possible.

Buy your drugs in country...

I have looked into Yellowdog, The Flyshop, etc, but I want to see if there is a less expensive way to do it.

Yes, but then you will have no one to bitch to about the shitty accommodations, broken air conditioner, dog food they call meals, and the fact that your house is actually a grass palapa with spiders the size of your palm that like to climb into your mouth and take a shit when you are asleep...

I was hoping that I could just rent some cool lil' cabana and just pay a local guide for a day.

Okay Flip...You want a light wind and the fish coming at a 70 degree angle too?...

MEXICO RETURNS

I have planned a ton of trips in the past, but they have always been all fishing.

Oh, so you never had sex before...Now you know what everyone's been talking about...

want to make sure we both have a great time without sacrificing the happiness of the other.

Are you SURE you're hetero?...Come on dude, if you're happy, it just comes to pass that she'll be happy...I mean, if she really loves you...Right?...

Good..High-five...You're fishing like a fiend, and sex is anytime, anywhere, anyhow...Cause you'll be the only one conscious...

Have any of you done the research on a trip like this and got any advice on where, when (I am going sometime between November - January) and how?

Oh, here I can help you out...Turneffe Island Lodge is great, but best saved for when your father in-law is paying for it...I'd suggest you start in Belize City...Take a Taxi to Albert Street, which goes right by the water taxi's...On the north side of the bridge, is a little mall of sorts...More like a shitload of shops separated by hanging towels, but run by a man named Renaldo, who has a bit of a lazy eye and always has hit pet monkey with him...The monkey is friendly, and will immediately befriend your fiance'...It's part of the scam to get you to pay $10 to get her picture taken holding a monkey...You'll also notice the monkey is wearing what looks like a shock collar, but in reality, it's a web camera...And you'll notice the monkey is always standing under your fiance's skirt...Well, Renaldo makes the real money on http://www.upskirtourists.com, but back to fishing....

Hand Renaldo $10 and ask him where you can find Gilbert's Taco Stand...He'll point you in the right direction...and e-mail the upskirt video to your blackberry for $20...Gilbert is a good shit, speaks good English and besides running the taco stand also has a porn shop and a ferry service...Oh, and whatever you do, don't let him talk you into going into the porn shop...

One of the things you never hear about Belize is that the city has a HUGE midget population...They're basically looked down upon by the culture as impure, so the only business they can prosper in is Internet Porn...You know, naked midget wrestling...midget dog sex, midget fisting...the stuff you're always look at on the computer at work...Anyway, they have this one midget named Lillio...And he's hung like a mule...

Lillio is always walking around the shop naked...And he has this habit of standing next to women and letting his Johnson rest on their foot...And I can GUARANTEE Lillio is going to proposition your lady...And here's the problem with that...Your standard midget porn video like Valley of the Trolls or Snow White and the Seven Gangbangs pays the woman around $10K...And you'll be thinking that you can go to Turneffe Island Lodge on that day's work...But keep in mind that Lillio's nickname is "The Log Splitter", and I'll say no more...

Anyway, if you go in the porn shop, Lillio will be hassling you to let her do the shoot, while dragging his dick repeatedly across her foot, and it'll be enough to likely warp her senses to the point that she will never want to have a man stand naked in front of her again... And did I mention that You are the one who drank the wedded bliss Cool-Aid?...

Tell Gilbert you want to catch the ferry out to Isla Turneffe and stay at McKay's place...It's about $30 each, $25 if you're willing to sit with a chicken cage on your lap...But it's safe, and Gilbert will wash the droppings off your feet when you get to the dock at Isla Turneffe...McKay will be at the dock with his staff unloading the chicken crates, and he'll give you a ride on the truck to the lodging... Did I mention that McKay owns one of the largest poultry farms/ factories in Belize?...No biggie, cause the house is phenomenal... It's made out of Mahogany with giant living trees woven through the rooms with 20-foot ceilings, and lush tropical gardens…It really is a great place to lay low if you were an ex-smuggler/CIA Op that got caught ferrying human kidneys into Cuba…

Anyway, make yourselves at home…McKay will have all the spliff and heroin you might want, but you'll have to get your GHB and Non-Barbituate hypnotics at any pharmacia in Belize City…There's always a ton of employees walking around the grounds, and there's a big beach right out front with a handful of hammocks hanging from palm trees…Hop in a hammock with your lady, and ask one of the employees to grab you guys a couple of queer boy frozen drinks and you're set…

Oh, a couple of words of caution…First off, don't have sex in the hammocks…well, unless you're into walking the edge of beastiality… And don't get me wrong here, after all, who isn't…But once you get a little of that GHB into her, you'll be thinking about knocking a quick one out, so why not in the hammock…Well, Sheeba is always around…And besides being a giant female German Shephard and McKay's guard dog, Sheeba…well…Sheeba has a thing for the L-A-D-I-E-S…And…well, you know…you're going to be looking for that threesome…so…

The problem is that Sheeba won't announce her presence…She'll wait in the shadows until you get to business….then she'll sneak up quietly…crawl under your lady…And…Start licking through the weave of the hammock…And did I mention, that it's a pretty big weave…

And it feels GOOD…Well, so I've heard…

She'll start on your lady's butt and work her way around the world… until you get into the fold…Once that happens….Well, you'll just have to have it again…And there's nothing more pitiful than a guy hooked on guy/girl/dog /hammock sex…

Anyway, you'll love the big king size canopy beds, the fresh fruit and juices, the gourmet meals that McKay's chef cooks up…And every evening around 6 p.m., they throw all the parts from the butchered chickens into the water at the dock, and watching those giant fucking sharks come in there and eat chicken heads is unreal... If you get stoned with McKay, he might even break out a few thermite grenades or phosphorous bombs and let you pitch them into the water and watch the shark parts fly...It's pretty fucking fun...

Oh, and there's a shitload of bonefish right on the beach in front of McKays, or you can take his Maverick HPX around the corner to the Central Lagoon and chase permit, tarpon and schools of bones...Bring a six weight and a nine weight rod and tan Crazy Charlies and ghost crab flies and you're set...

Thanks in advance.... oh... and tight lines, screaming reels and what are they biting on?

De Nada...See above...

In-Laws

in-laws
Alteredstates

how's everyone doing with extra family in town? curious to hear anyone's interesting experiences this year or last.

this morning had a bit of a blow up with my girlfriend's parents. i have been living with this girl for 2 years, we are both 28. her parents are very traditional and both her and i are not in the slightest. we are liberal no doubt, especially when it comes to marriage, etc. anyways, we have gotten the "when are you 2 getting married" in the past from her mom but always laughed it off. this AM though she came at us guns blazing, "why arent you married? you are embarassing the family by living together, if you wait too long to have children they'll come out retarded." just some real selfish mean-spirited things. i held my tongue the best i could considering if it weren't her parents i'd have bit some heads off. i dont expect them to have our same beliefs or opinions, but fuck, cant they just be happy for the two of us, we are in a super good place right now and i'm just tired of the bullshit. and on xmas???? really???? anyways, i remained unscathed, but the GF was in tears and the tension was there and huge. such a clusterfuck, i really need to get out on the water. times like these i wish i had some fishable business within stomping distance.

anyone else with good family, inlaw stories? i'm sure they are out there.

Well shit, if everyone's going to ante up, I guess I'll throw my two nickels in...I'm not sure what you expected from the gf's mom, but keep in mind that you are wearing out her daughter's ginae with no financial commitment, so mom is thinking you can wake up tomorrow and think, "What was I thinking? I like redheads, not brunettes," and can be nailing the office slut while her daughter is left with another suitcase of marrow to put in her closet and just a little more mental instability from having to stick her finger in your butt when she's giving you a blow job along with the thought of you still having those pictures of her getting herself off with a shoe horn...So mom is just being a mom, knowing you're coercing her daughter down the path of filth, flour and fisting, without having to buy into the dream house and 3.2 kids scheme to at least leave her daughter with all your worldly possessions and a lifetime of financial debt and ruination...

As I see it, there's only a couple of ways around the issue...

A.) You can sell off a rod and purchase a promise ring at a pawn shop or in the classifieds so you don't have to pay the full nut, which should buy you another 18 months of bendovers and a dry spot to sleep in...Then formulate a plan to get mom out of the picture...

B.) Plead poverty, and get mom to buy a ring and send the two of you off on an engagement trip to some romantic destination like the Louisiana marsh where you can spend the day sight casting reds and the nights trying to wear a hole in her fallopian tubes, knowing full well you can break it off at any time and still get out of it financially sound and mentally retarded...

C.) Tell mom you haven't decided what it is you want in life, a sweet young wife or her dirty, hot, sexy mom with a shaved beavee who likes to stick her finger up your butt when she's giving you a bj...

D.) Act like you don't understand what the problem is, you're thinking about getting a job, but until then you need her daughter to support your fishing bum lifestyle in the fashion you've become accustomed to, and she should appreciate that you contribute to the relationship by taking care of her daughter's freaky sexual issues, particularly those involving soft plastics, and if she doesn't believe you, you can show her a picture you carry in your wallet of her daughter with a plastic trolling squid sticking out of her butt...

Well it's not like I can tell him the truth...You know, that he's already heading down the path of righteous familial Cool Aid...It won't be long before he buys into that crap she tells him...You know, that he's funny and witty, and how she loves his sarcasm...How she buys into the sex in public places, tells him his Johnson is "SO BIG", and that she always cums by making that frown...

And he'll drink the Cool Aid...And that sex any time...Well, that's been cut back a bit...and the public places thing....Well, "I'm not that drunk"...and BTW, you need to go into the bathroom and take a full shower and shave, brush your teeth and trim that nasty junk up a bit before I'm going to have anything to do with it, and if you're lucky, and fast enough about it, I might still be awake, in the mood and it might be your birthday...Or you can just buy me something really nice and I'll have missionary sex with you--that is, if you get it over with quickly...

And you'll still be buying into that marital bliss theory that her mother helps reinforce by telling you that you should get a second job, so the two of you can have a nicer house, and you can go on expensive vacations to all those places that her daughter has always wanted to visit, you know, like Tuscany and Prague and a handful of other shitholes that are so remotely removed from anything you like to do (like fish), that getting laid will be the only salvation to the trip, which for some reason always coincides with her menstrual cycle,, but with enough whining and pouting you eventually pull a bj out of it, because after all, you're only ponying up the $8K...Oh, and because you'll be jumping at every opportunity to make some extra money to finance the trips and your wife's 40 pairs of jeans, 70 pairs of shoes and all the accessories that she'll always tell you, "Oh no, that's not new, I've worn that a bunch of times" to make you feel like a smendrick for asking, you'll have to give up all the things you like to do under the guise that she is the only one who ever makes any sacrifices around here...So essentially, your fishing gear is now relegated to stuff you walk out into the garage and tinker with when you're so pissed off at her you want to strangle her and leave her in a shopping cart on her mom's porch with her ass in the air and a 30 inch replica of the Leaning Tower of Pisa sticking out of her butt...

But no, you work your ass off, never get laid, and you're not fucking funny or witty, and would you please stop that boring, irritating sarcasm that is the second worse thing she has always hated about you, the worst being your inability to satisfy her sexual needs with that little "Thing" of yours...But she'll put up with it, missionary, on your birthday, Christmas and anniversary, and maybe one other special occasion during the year when you "Buy her something nice like tickets for a lovely vacation in Bosnia...And you no longer get to sleep on that side of the bed, and don't even think about planting your lazy ass on the couch and watching football all afternoon, and isn't there some laundry or other housework to do, you know I work too? although it's only part time, 8 hours a week...

And then one day she'll wake up horny as hell, wanting sex, and even some of that nasty stuff we did when we were living together... Only it'll be with someone, fuck, anyone, but you...And mom will reinforce the effort by mentioning that she always thought you were an underachiever and that she could tell by looking at your small feet that you'd never be able to satisfy her daughter's needs, so she should just keep the house and her BMW, and kick you and your 1999 Toyota Pick-up to the curb, and oh, isn't that Italian guy at the shoe store hot?...

California

What are my options CA peoples?
NICH

I'll be headed to Yosemite National Park 5/14 - 5/18. I'll be with the lady friend and her family but I'll be fishing 3 of those days... Any fishing info would be greatly appreciated and if if any of y'all crazies want to meet up I'd be down for that as well. Shoot me a PM if you aren't hip on the whole world listening in

Thanks in advance,
Nick

Ahhhh…Where do I start…When you hit the park, you'll see the "Speeding Kills Bears" signs everywhere bears have been previously hit by cars…Those are usually locations you'll regularly see bears on the side of the road, so if you've got a paintball gun in the car, this is really a good time to put it in the trunk…Cause you know what's going to happen…You can't spliff up b'cause mommasita senorita and pappa nazi are in the front, and they not only think you're too porkchop for their daughter, and thus don't like you worth a fart, but also are looking for a reason to push you off the side of a cliff and say you jumped, so you'll probably be dropping peyote buds and doing whippets every time they look forward just to maintain posture...And you know how three good peyote buds gets the light posts looking like one solid florescent bulb when cruising down the road, but four peyote buds generally lead to an unexplained loss of a couple of hours in the day--at least when no one has a video camera for the rehash...And there really is nothing funnier than dotting pink across a walking brown rug... But trust me when I say this, those park rangers have zero sense of humor...And if you're somewhere up on a peak when they pull the car over after chasing you around a few bends...And when the park ranger walks up and asks why your gf's dad didn't pull over right away, you'll probably put on the hat and moustache, lean out the window and say, "Cause Ya Didn't say WHOA...If'n you want us to stop you should say, "When I say Whoa, I mean W-H-O-A!!!"... And then dot their khaki outfits with pink kisses...Which will get them to step to the passenger window, point at the paintball gun as ask, "Who the hell are you?"...and you just know, "For any one of you lilly livered bow legged varmits care the slap leather with me, in case any of ya get any idears, ya better know yer dealin with. I'm tha' hootiness, tootiness, shootiness bob tailed wild cat in the west. I'm tha' fastest gun north, south, east, and west of tha' pecos" is gonna come out of your mouth...And dood, it's all downhill from there... Just saying...

In all seriousness though...You want to fish in the Red Valley, which is six or seven miles below Yosemite Falls...You'll see the pullover and the path through the woods...It's downhill most of the way, and a bitch of a walk back up after fishing all day...The path isn't well marked, and you'll come to a spot where there's a little hand pump for a well where you can get a drink of water and rest, Cause it's about a two mile hike to the best water...Keep in mind that the trail goes to the left side at the water hole...

You don't want to continue downhill there, cause that's the old water trail for the Miwok (pronounced Mee-Wok) tribe of California Indians. Of all the Native Americans in this country, the Miwok's are supposedly the most beautiful...And there's still a bunch of them around in that valley...So if you take the trail, you'll likely

MEXICO RETURNS

come to an opening by a stream where Itahanni lives…Itahanni is S-M-O-K-I-N-G H-O-T!!!..I mean for a 30-year old….She's got that long jet black hair and i-n-c-r-e-d-i-b-l-e cheekbones…And a butt that pops when she walks…And she's sweet as sugar…But…

Did I mention that Itahanni loosely translated means nympho clown werewolf?…It's true…And if you get close to her, you'll be totally mesmerized by how beautiful her skin is….It's the smoothest, creamiest, wholesomest skin you've ever seen…And Itahanni likes to cook a lot, so she'll likely be hanging out by the fire and will ask you to join her for lunch…Whatever you do, don't eat anything… First off, there's this fried stuff she makes that looks like calamari, but is actually Ruby Mountain Lizard rings, which besides tasting outstanding are the Native American version of natural Viagra, only times infinity…And then there's the sandwiches which are made on real wheat bread, with venison strips cooked down in a natural truffle and scallion/carrot sauce, which rocks, but the lettuce she puts on there is a fairly rare native shrub called Stiff weed, which has some kind of neurotoxin in it that will paralyze you in about two minutes…

And the next thing you know, you're laying on a table…Naked… with your pecker sticking in a hole that you originally thought was an umbrella stand…and if you could see from below, you'd know why, cause you've got the woodiest woodpecker north, south, east and west of the Paco's…

Now if'n you did your research, you know the Miwok's have such beautiful skin because they constantly rub it with a lotion they make out of semen, aloe rinds and saliva…which they keep in a big, hollowed-out gourd…And, well…Did I mention that Itahanni was S-M-O-K-I-N-G H-O-T?…Well, it's because of the lotion…And did I mention that it takes a LOT of lotion to keep those looks going?…And, well, Itahanni is a woman…And She's 30 dood… Which means she's concerned about here looks fading…So whether you like it or not, dood, you're a lotion donor…

The Miwok's used to raise cattle, so they're experts at milking…

So Itahanni is going to get under that table and milk you… Repeatedly…And here the thing about the Ruby Mountain Lizards, that shit takes about 10 hours to wear off, so I don't know where Viagra comes up with the '6 hour see a doctor limit', cause it's a solid 10 hours of swinging lumber…and therein lies the problem… After the first hour or so, you're probably going to run dry, so she'll be wanting to give you a dirty Miwok, which is where she dips her hand in Beaver fat, stick two fingers in your butt, gets your prostate between them and squeezes as she gives you a reach-around…And that's not the worst part…

When she's done, she's going to want to sample the cream, so she'll be rubbing it all over herself, particularly on her face…and…well…. She's gonna want to thank you…And…Well, Eskimo's aren't the only tribe known for rubbing noses…

So in the long run, after you produce a certain quantity she'll get you some raw cactus juice to drink, which while tasting like Earth, it does get the taste of beauty cream out of your mouth…And if you're lucky, she'll let you fish the stream that runs through her property, which is closed to everyone except Native Americans and chock full of fat wild fish…

So by the time you make it back to the car, you'll be jazzed from the action, although you'll have the extreme tent-pitching in the front of your pants to explain around to your girlfriend's parents…Then again, you'll probably have a couple hours left of the Ruby Mountain Lizard rings if you can get your girlfriend in an accommodating mood…

Oh, and your face will look like a baby's bottom come morning… So you have that going for you NICH…

Islamorada

Fishing 90 miles from Key West
Ajax16

Between Cuba and the Caymans are the world's largest protected archipeligo. Within 70 miles offshore of Cuba are the los Jardines de la Reina. This location is reserved for catch & release fishers & divers. Let us know of your interests.

Dood....You seem like a solid Drakian...So I'm going to shoot you in the right direction...Just don't tell anyone where you learned all this stuff or I'll loose my mojo status...

Islamorada is a blast, and it looks like you're locked and loaded... Couple of things you should know first though...

There's a TON of hotels, each with their own amenities...But you want to stay at the Holiday Isle...Trust me on this...Right outside your door are the "A Docks" for Islamorada...All the bigtime guides and captains work out of the Holiday Isle Marina...So you'll have the inside scoop on what's biting the whole time there...

They're also very cool...Islamorada's economy is based on tourism, so everywhere you go there is a local's price and a tourist price...

Likewise, they treat the locals different than the tourists...Years ago, they figured out a way to tell who was a local from a tourist—they developed a secret code...Everywhere you go, you want to use the password at the end of your sentence or when addressing someone, and thus they'll know you're a local and will cut you huge discounts and get you into some macking parties, etc...

The password is: Jagoff...Use it liberally...Like when you order a drink..."I'd like a Patrone Margarita Jagoff"...Or, "Can you please bring me a menu, Jagoff?"...The people will pretend to be insulted, which is their way of telling you "we're cool" while keeping anyone within earshot who might have heard the password of stealing and using it themselves...It's a very tight club...

Now I know you've heard how tough the fishing is in Islamorada, but that's just on the bay side...On the ocean side, the bonefish and tarpon action is hand-over-fist...And for most of us traveling on a budget, we can't afford a guide...You're best bet is to slide over to World Wide Sportsman and grab a small raft from the pool toy section...These work great because they get you out to the fish people can't pressure from land...AND, since you're at the Holiday Isle Marina, you should ask one of the charter captains to save you a couple of barracudas from their day on the water...Trust me, they catch a lot of them, and it's no imposition...Don't forget to use the Jagoff password... You want three or four big barracudas for bait...

No one will tell you this, but bonefish can't pass up a hunk of barracuda...Shoot, the locals will deny it and even say you're crazy, but on when they go fishing, that's what they use for bait...Remind them that you're in the know by reiterating that you're a Jagoff... Barracuda chunks are so effective, they won't use it for charters because you'd catch so many fish, you'd wipe them out...But the barracuda has to be f-r-e-s-h...So you can put them in the fridge in your hotel room over night...Don't put them in the cooler, because the fresh water from the melting ice will spoil them....Then again, every Jagoff knows that...

On the south end of Islamorada are three bridges...You want to launch at the middle bridge, and make sure the tide is flowing east towards the ocean, which to you means towards where the sun comes up...The best way to keep those cudas fresh is to hang them in the water off a short piece of rope...Think about it, that's the temperature they live in every day, and they don't spoil...Anyway, hop in your raft, push out toward the bridge and cut yourself a small piece of barracuda and bait up...Hang the rest over the side...It usually takes about 20 minutes for the bite to turn on, but trust me, it will...

By the end of the day, you'll be so tired from reeling in bonefish and tarpon that you'll want to move to Islamorada and become a permanent Jagoff...That is, if you aren't already...And don't spend your entire day chasing bonefish and tarpon...Save some time to hit the sandbar just outside Holiday Isle...It's T-O-P-L-E-S-S... And full of smoking hot, horny, porn star babes...Who love to have their pictures taken...By anyone, but particularly someone without a tan, covered in oil and wearing cutoff jeans with the zipper down... Remind them that you're a Jagoff, and you'll likely get invited to climb into their 90-foot sportfishing boat with a half dozen ladies down below...It's like living in a dream, and it happens every day on that sandbar...One minute you're gawking tanned meat pillows, and the next you're a Jagoff in a porn movie...

And that's just your first day in Islamorada...

You haven't been to the Lor-e-leir yet...Or Woodies...Or any of the other local hot spots...

Shoot, I'll even help you other there...You know how the Lor-e-leir got it's name?...It used to be called Lor-e's Landing after the owner's girlfriend...Then he caught her stepping out in the parking lot, and she denied it even though he had proof on video tape... So he dumped her and changed the name to Lor-e-Leir to let the whole world know what happened...It's true...Shoot, the local Jagoff's know it, but you can impress people at the bar and get the bartender to buy your drinks if you tell the story repeatedly...It's part of the rule the owner made when he changed the name...Every time someone tells the story, they drink free...Don't forget to end the story with, "I'll take a free drink, Jagoff"...

Oh, and if you decide to go to Key West for the day...The Password is: Anus Breath...

Jamaica

HELP Fly-fishing in Jamaica???
fishnut08

Heading to Jamaica in March to FlyFish!?? No clue who I can contact????

Im looking for some help as I am headed to Jamaica to Vacation (fish) with my lovely lady in March. I haven't found a lick of info on fly-fishing and need a little background info in order to even explore the waters on my own. I'm really not into the idea of dragging my fly gear down there with the possibility of it getting ripped off if I have no idea where to start. Anyone have any ideas or contacts of where I could start, I would be greatly appreciative.

Who wants to look at the ocean or sit on a fishing charter for $1000 a day! Not me..... Please help. I'll send you some rum in exchange!

Thanks a million,
Chris
Denver, CO

D ood, first off, you're welcome…Love Jamaica, but not allowed to go there any more… Kind of a non-requested governmental understanding…So let's see, you'll need to go shopping before you go. You'll need:…

(12) limes.
(1) copy of the most recent Vince Flynn or Stephen Hunter novel.
(1) bottle Milagro tequila (blue bottle)
(2) tins Coleman's dry mustard.
(1) large bottle Astroglide—Don't get Wet, or KY or any other derivative or you'll be sorry…

I'm not sure where you're going, likely Ocho Rios, Kingston or Montego Bay, but when you get there you'll realize that most of the fish have already been harvested for food… That being said, there's a killer cove in Port Esquivel which is in Clarendon Parish--a part of Middlesex County on the south central area of the island…It's owned by Bugsy Clemonts, an old friend from when I was flying "hurricane tracker" planes over Cuba…

Bugsy has about eight miles of coastline there…Very private stuff…armed guards…people mysteriously disappearing, etc… But the cove is pristine, and loaded with turbot, bonefish, tarpon and snappers!…oh, and Stone Crabs!…It's called Rush Cove, and on a few of the maps…Shallow hard-bottom flats, but you'll want wading boots because the coral sand can be a bitch…

When you pack, put everything from the list in your suitcase, or it'll get glipped at customs…Put the limes in a bag on the top, and when you get to customs and the Customs Master opens your suitcase, pull out the bag of limes and say, "I didn't realize you can't bring these into Jamaica. Would you like them?"...They can't get good limes there, and the Customs Master will immediately let you and everyone else in your party through...

I don't know where you're staying, but what you'll want to do is either take a rental or hop a Jimmy Cab down to Maya City, and from there go to Brownie Ahul's place...Jimmy Cabs are red, black and white checkered, and usually vans...Jamaica is a big ass island, and it can be pricy, but tell them you want to go to Brownie Ahul's...It'll run about $14, or basically you pay for gas...Psst—Brownie and Bugsy are what is known as major players on the Island and everyone is afraid of them, so if you know them, you are safe at all times...In fact, if you're trying to buy some pot from a marketdweeb and he pulls a knife, just say, "Fuck, my friend Brownie Ahul isn't going to like this," and that guy will shake like a mofo before he runs off...

Brownie owns a fruit/meat pie/prostitution stand that has the best of all of the above on the island...He's also Bugsy's brother and an avid reader...When you get to Brownie's, tell him you know MEXICO from the old days...He'll know what you're talking about...hand him the book you brought... From then on, it's anything you want....Sugar Cane, meat pies, 16-year old meat pies...free...Take advantage of it, and don't be an asshole, ugly American and ask for two girls because Brownie's girls are pretty well-trained as it is, and after getting beaved into paste with the bead-pull ending, you'll be glad there isn't a second coming...

Anyway, be sure to let Brownie know you want to fish Rush Cove...He'll call Karina, Bugsy's girlfriend who will come pick you up. Karina is from Belgium, speaks with that Euro sex freak accent, and is a smoking hot blonde...I'm 50, so Karina must be about 32 now...Be careful, she LOVES Americans...

Unfortunately, Bugsy hates people thumping his old lady, so walk that polite sport flirting/not in a hundred million years times eternity would I fuck you line and everyone will be happy...

Last time I was there Karina drove a Ferrari, but I believe she's now into Lotus' and has a new Tesla, so she'll swing by Brownie's to get you in that...What you need to know before you meet Bugsy is that he's a full-blown Rastafarian, and that he has a gummie eye--You know, the milky dead eye thing you see every now and then down there...He actually got it from Karina, who used to date Ziggy Marley and stabbed bugsy in eye with fork, but that's another story...

Karina is a bit of an exhibitionist and will have nothing on but a thong...no top, so expect it...Don't stare!...Give her the bottle of tequila...Besides being a major league tequila drinker, Karina has a bunch of bottle trees, which you'll see the minute you hit the property...They have all kinds of bottles hanging from them to ward the spirits off, and blue is the most difficult colored bottle to find...So you just killed two birds with one stone and made Karina your friend as well, which is good because she'll be the one who monitors your pulse if you get into the Lambs Bread...

Don't let all the machine guns, dogs, etc on the property bother you...It's a poor nation, so sometimes people do desperate things and trespass on Bugsy's land...And those people have to be dealt with or the global spliff economy will take a hit, if you know what I mean...But they're no threat to you...Being a "Glower" (their term for white man), and showing up with Karina, they'll do anything not to piss you off because they've seen what happens when Bugsy gets mad...

Bugsy is actually a cool dude, full on skinny ass black guy with a great sense of humor and creepy dreads...He and Brownie and I did a little thinning of the heard in Grenada before we officially were "in country," and they owe me big time...Bugsy can party like a rock star, so when he offers, don't even think of it, or you'll wake up five weeks later smelling like vagina with a beard full of peanut butter and a Welcome to Jamaica Have A Nice Day tattoo across your ass...Just tell him you are a friend of mine, and I told you to look him up if you wanted to fish while there...Then hand him the two tins of mustard... That will get you a corn tooth smile from Bugsy...

Rush Cove is full of stone crabs, and Bugsy is a stone crab eating mofo, but you can't get Coleman's mustard in Jamaica... And Coleman's is the bomb daddy when it comes to making your own mustard sauce...Bugsy will be so farking happy, he'll stuff your backpack will everything from hash oil and space cakes to the ooey-gooey, which will be rolled into the biggest joint you have ever seen...My suggestion is that you dump all that shit the second you get off the property, but most people have to learn the hard way...

Be sure to ask Bugsy for some whitecrab flies...That's the local pattern that the fish can't pass up...Bugsy has a bunch because Karina's sister Katya has a business using locals to tie them and sell them everywhere from Curacao to San Pedro... Be sure to get the #4's, because the #2's have a shitty hook in them that straightens out on anything over 8 pounds...Bugsy will load you up, fill you full of food and drink and point you down the trail to Rush Cove...He'll also make sure you have your Astroglide with you...

It's only about a half mile walk, but you have to go through the mud bogs, so you can't wear your shoes or wading boots because they'll get suctioned off...You'll know when you hit the bogs because the mud looks like it's dry and cracked, but that's just on the surface…It's still damp underneath, and it's a bit of a pain to walk through it, but it's only about 300 yards and it doesn't take long…Now here's the important thing… Stop before you cross the bogs and cover your feet, ankles and legs all the way up to your kneecap with Astroglide…

The mud is home to the Wool Worms, which are these little bug-looking worms that stick to the hair and skin on your legs and then lay eggs in your skin, the hatchlings which dig trains through your body until they hit an organ and decide to hang out and eat…The Astroglide keeps the Wool Worms from adhering to your skin and hair and kills any that touch it…Be sure to save enough for the trip back, because the water will wash it all off…

Anyway, the trail comes out in the middle of Rush Cove…I like the stuff to the left, although it has less fish but more bones over 10 pounds…Also, there's a river mouth about 400 yards down that always has 30-40 pound tarpon rolling in it…And they love the hell out of those white crabs…Also, watch for mutton snapper crossing the flat—they're usually so big they have to swim on their sides, and look like a big orange platter moving through the water…Oh, and watch for low-flying planes…Farking Cubans like to sneak in and take a shot everyone once in a while, and they figure any Glower on Bugsy's land is a target of opportunity…

There's a few sharks and barracuda, but not anything you have to worry about while fishing…If you see someone walking the beach, just ignore them unless they wave you in…If that happens, it usually means Bugsy has sent someone with food (usually shrimp cocktail and stone crabs) and cold beer… You'll know, because again, she's going to be a young and hot brown skin wearing less cotton than you'll find in the top of an aspirin bottle…Lunch is on Bugsy, eat, drink and partake all you want…Just tell the lovely what you like, dislike, and always wondered about and she'll accommodate…You'll want to take a nap, but don't or you'll miss the afternoon bite…

And don't even think of taking a hit on that cartoonish giant cigar spliff or eating one of those cakes…You think you're bad, but you don't know bad until you grow up eating rats and wiping your ass with palm leaves…You do that for 20 years and you'll know how to escape…For instance, Karina is going to use that tequila to cook with…Yeah, she wants it to take the nasty taste out of the mescaline drops she makes every other Thursday…And in case I didn't mention it, don't go there on Thursday, or you'll see the giant bats…Fish until about 4:30, and then head back to the house…It's a solid 20 fish day…Be sure to Astroglide up before you cross the mud…

Karina's girlfriends will likely be showing up around the pool when you get back…Just play it cool, don't stare (yes, those are obscenely giant basketball-sized titties on the ginger) and yes it's very nice of them to ask you to go for a swim…It's a ploy to start the party, and you're the party favor…Just be cool, thank Bugsy and Karina and ask for a ride back to town… Soon as you get in your car head out of town and when you see a pull off dump the Krippi and head for the hotel…If you came by Jimmie Cab, wait until you get to the hotel and dump the Krippi in the garbage can or the driver will spin back and pick it up after he drops you off and that usually leads to a loss of cabbies on the island…Be sure you don't dump it in a garbage can on the property, because they burn the garbage there, and you can KO the entire property for about 10 hours with what Bugsy will likely give you…

And lastly, you'll likely still have some Astroglide left and your babe waking from her nap…So you'll have that going for you…

Taho

Hackle Harem.
AftonAngler

I'm flush...

Kind of feel like Booger from Better Off Dead...where he realizes what the street value of the mountain is...

Bird Brains...thats what this boils down to...I have something like 100 saddles...all dripping with the long hackles that these chicks crave...they are willing to pay up to $5 PER FEATHER!

Me and Lucky are going up to Tahoe this weekend with dimebags of Euro Hackle...set up shop and see what kind of favors and cashola we can extract

Mexico...how would you do it? Help a brotha out...

Tahoe is a crazy ass place...At least King's Beach is...if you come in on 431, right before it hits 267 there's a small yellow building with a sign that says, "North Country Spiritualist" and "readings, visitations and guidance"...That's Nadine Minton's place...

Besides looking like Gwyneth Paltrow with giant fake tits, Nadine is a spirit guide and all that creepy afterworld crap...Her place abuts about 65,000 acres that push against Lake Tahoe and towards the Nevada line...Stop in and get your palm read...She'll know why you're there and that you know me...Yes, it's weird, but you haven's seen anything yet...Wait until it gets freaky...

Anyway, besides being one of those Earth children, Nadine is also an heir to the Motts Apple fortune, so she has about 600 million or so in the bank...So that black Ford F650 out front is hers... If you notice, there's a giant tree behind the building that looks like it's been there for 150 years...It has...And here's where the weirdness starts...Nadine lives in the tree...if you look closer, you can see the little rooms, floors and roofs built under the canopy... That's her house dude...She gets in it by parking that F650 under the tree and climbing onto the roof and grabbing a branch...So good luck there...

Despite being an arrogant biatch, Nadine does have some manners, and because she knows you know me, she'll ask you to stay over... It's cool...Don't drink too much, cause it's a long way down...Also, that 65,000 acres behind her building...Well, that's hers....And her sister Lilly's...It's got some great streams that run along the railroad tracks...Lots of browns, rainbows...Lots of good stuff and all private...Just ask, she'll let you fish it...

Little background on Nadine...She's brilliant...Used to be an engineer...But not a lot of women driving trains these days...But if you look at the big garage next to the building, you'll see railroad tracks coming out of the south door...She's got her own locomotive and railway on the property, and it runs right along the best holes in the rivers...One day, she had an epiphany and moved into space... Also, she and her sister like to visit the pipe...And I'm not talking pot or hash...She'll hit the opium every now and then, and that's when you see her darker side...

Her sister Lily is a total freak show...Literally...And you'll know that the second you meet her...And not just because she's only four feet tall...(P.S. don't use the word midget or even little person around her, or she'll grab your nuts and squeeze them to bring you down to her size)...Anyway, Lily has a black corvette with a bumper sticker that says, "If you can beat me, you can eat me," and always wears something leather...So you know where that's going...

Friday and Saturday are the nights when the girls hit the pipe…
Don't be there…And if you are, don't partake…And whatever you
do, don't try out the SWING…I know the swing looks crazy and
like a bunch of fun, but it's not, it's a dungeon…Once you get
strapped in, you can't get loose…And that's where it'll all turn
weird…

Nadine can obviously have any man she wants…And let me tell
you, her charms are beyond the normal "oh my God, I think I blew
out a nut" charms…She's one hellofasexpot…And she LOVES her
baby (notice I didn't say little) sister…So once you get strapped in,
and particularly if you hit the pipe, Nadine and Lily are going to
take the swing for a spin…

Now normally Double A, I'm all for the double teaming sister
midget sex swing act, but that was until Lily asked me to suck on
her toes…Dude…Have you ever seen how small the feet are on
a four foot grown woman?…Man, that is just freaky…They're like
little baby feet…And trust me, once you get that little baby feet
thought into your mind, you can't get it out, not with the opium
pounding it back in…Its flacciddating…But don't think that will
get you out of it…Nadine will just jump on, and once you've yeasted
up, she'll hop off and it's back to Munchkin Land…

So as I was saying, dark memories…That shit freaked me out to
the point that I had to leave after three months…Still haunts me…
Freaky baby feet…Arrrgggghhhhhh….

So anyway, if'n you make it up there Sunday through Thursday,
Nadine will fire up the tank engine and drive you down to the river…
Shit, she'll even tell you what you're gonna want for dinner…It's
best not to even look at Lily…

Fishing will be good tho…And I slept like a bat in that tree…

Bahamas

freeport bahamas guide, not quite a TR, TR.
VAKU

So, I 'm going to be stuck in Freeport for a day in two weeks. Any one have a reco for a guide. I would much rather flail at bone fish for a few hours than take a cruise ship excursion.

Vaku, you seem a solid dude, so I'm going to hook you up... Okay, here's the thing about Freeport...On the nicest day of the year, the city proper is still the asshole of the world... But it's got the shits when it comes to great water...Problem is the locals that seem to have their hands held out at all times looking for Private Benjamin...Well, that and the dipshits that hawk everything from headache spliff to cornrows...But once you get around that, things can be pretty ire...

Before you leave the states, pick up an extra pair of quality sunglasses which are better than money when it comes to getting out of a pissing match...Doesn't hurt to get some Nancy Boy genie fishing pants either, as the doctor flies will take their penance in blood on the fishing grounds, which is a good excuse for blowing a cast, but those bites turn into oozing volcanoes later, which in the long run shuts down the hoochie momma time at night...

That shit being said, if you go to the Food Depot on Hwy 20 which is the grocery store the locals shop, grab a pack of Nutter Butters and get in the line with the white girl with dreads...That's Aggie Albury whose family has been there since boats only had sails...She'll ask you if you've got a craving...Tell her, "This always happens when I ride the vine"...She'll know you're down...

Tell her you're there on vacation, looking for the local hookup... She gets off at 10:00...Don't think that means you're getting off at 10:30...She doesn't play that game and will stick you in the ass with that giant pin/needle in her hair...And then you're fucked because Aggie is a cutter...and a poker, and you can bet there's some festering ass to mouth bacteria that will scare the shit out of penicillin on that cushion maker...

But if you play nicely nice, you might get an invite to wander down to Billie Joes, which is this funky local beach bar where her boyfriend Tevin Bishop tends the bar at night...Tevin is a stone cold killer, bout 6'5" and 240, 20 pounds of which are cajones, but he throws one mean fucking loop, the kind where you just step away in case he asks you to make one of your silly little humiliating half-haul casts...Fucker's dad was Christopher Bishop, a commercial fisherman who crashed a plane with six 50 gallon drums full of Quaaludes about 100 yards short of the runway...That was the plane in the trees you saw on the way in...

Anyway, Tevin's got a shack on the east end of the island, right at the end of the Grand Bahama Highway...And better yet, it's got a skiff...Even better, he owes me for sending him a batch of meds to take care of a mean case of impetigo he got while living on Moaning Joan's sailboat for two weeks...So tell him MEXICO said to look him up while you're there and he'd show you the golden bones...

Oh, one thing...Have some tact...Don't throw my name out right away...hang out, party a little, have a drink or ten, maybe even ask one of the girls at the bar to dance…And tip well…Let Tevin warm up to you before you play the IOU card, cause Tevin may be a solid dude but he doesn't like feeling like honky town is there to bend over the brown…

There will also likely be a tall skinny dude that's an exact double for Snoop Dog lying in the hammock on the left side of the bar… Don't stare, even when you see the comically giant joint in his hand…BTW, it is Snoop…Islanders call him Jimmy Right, cause he's always t-i-g-h-t…Again, don't fucking stare, cause if there's one thing the local's can't stand it's star fuckers and sweating the mainstream escapees is tantamount to begging for your own personal sandbar in your ass…Lastly, don't play the too cool card either and ask for a hit, cause the answer is already no…That's a personal Snoop rolled…

Around your fourth drink mention to Tevin that you heard he's the king of the golden bone…He'll know right away what you mean… And that you know me…He'll flash those pearlies with the biggest fucking corn tooth smile you ever saw…From there, you're in…

Come morning, Tevin will roll up to your hotel in his Land Rover with a dozen rods on the roof…Leave your gear at home, as he's got the Motts…Fucking handmade jewelry you can only dream of having in your hands…You'll head to the shack at the end of the Grand Bahama Highway, and rest assured they call it a Highway for a reason…It's a two joint, two beer ride…

You might luck out and he'll bring Aggie along…She doesn't fish, she likes to drop acid and wander around naked in the mangroves… Just a piece of advice so you don't spend too much time trying to cipher her ink and get caught staring…That butt hat tattoo in fancy cursive lettering says, "Deposits In Rear," leave it at that…Besides, even if you did get in, you'd never get the smell off…

Just play mesmerized deer caught in the headlights, take everything in, smoke and drink what's handed to you, don't talk much and get in the fucking boat…Tevin's likely to play the sweet tooth card and

break out some Bahamian candy as you pull away from the beach…
It's a green hard candy…Take it, palm it and pretend to put it into
your mouth…Whatever you do, don't fucking eat it, it's laced with
acid, the kind Tevin makes in his bathtub…

You see, while Tevin owes me a debt of gratitude, he doesn't
particularly want you to remember how to ever again get to where
he takes you, and he knows the acid will either make you one funny
American douche doing pirouettes on the flats or a locked down,
closed mouth cloud-riding sword fighter…Be the second, it's easier
to fake…And make no mistake, Tevin and Aggie ate the candy, but
they're pretty used to its thump, so they'll just be funny as shit and
the perfect hosts, although Tevin does like to play pinball with the
blacktip sharks on the run and they do tend to leap from the water
when the prop goes up their ass, so watch for the flying bags of
sandpaper with teeth…

You have to cross four cuts in the island, 100 yard wide openings in
the land that go completely through to the other side and provide a
flushing effect…Stay away from those cuts at all times, cause when
the current gets moving you can turn into a Treasure Cay drifter in
no time and there's a gauntlet of tiger sharks you'll have to run to
hit Treasure Cay, but just after the fourth cut is 1,500 yards of sand,
urchins and these little fucking sponges that are full or purple ink
that will turn your soles purple as a drunk Viking's fan…

The first thing you'll notice is that the current there is going out
of the cut, not into it, and that the water is brown, not the flats of
azure you're used to seeing…That's because the water is coming
out of the marsh where the red mangrove leaves fall into the water
and decay, turning the water brown…Tis no big deal, and really the
key to the whole process…The water in the marsh flows in from
one of the other cuts and washes out the stained water and about
100,000 bonefish…

There's a hump of sand in the middle of the bowl and Tevin will
push the boat on the sand, toss out and anchor grab a rod and
wander off without saying shit…That's your key to pick a rod and

head in the opposite direction, cause if you hang near him you won't be able to fool him with your fake bathtub acid high...Work the edge of the bowl in eight to ten inches of water, lead the fish by 20 feet and let them come to the fly and by all means don't make a strip more than four inches...The bones will do the rest...Watch for blacktips which have an inane ability to sneak up on your ass 105 from behind and will steal your calf, which means you bleed out while a giant black dude and a naked white chick laugh like hell at the half moon that used to be your lower leg...

When you catch a bone, check it out, instead of being silver, they've got a golden tint to them from the tannic acid in the marsh...It's pretty fucking special...It might help to hold one up and yell, "Fuck me, I snagged my pocket watch," which will help with the fake acid high ruse...

One last bit of advice...Don't wander too far from the boat...Tevin and Aggie make this trip together regularly, but they also tend to get so loopy that they forget anyone joined them and will leave your ass sprinting curses across the sand...If that happens, just find a shark and get it over with, cause the no seeums and mosquitos will surely pot your mind while sucking you dry like a hooker with 20 piercings in her tongue...

Catch a shitpot of fish of a lifetime, laugh like a mother fucker and fall down a lot, and when everyone heads for the boat be the first one there...You won't have to fake the Bahamian bathtub acid high on the way back as you'll likely be flushing the memories and laughing out loud like a mofo...It's all cool...Happens to everyone...

On the ride back, don't let Tevin talk you into stopping for a cup of conch ceviche at Macky's...While the conch ceviche is spectacular, Macky's is where the Russian girls who are trying to get to America are paying off their debt, and that shit's going to go bad, as in dick in the sand bad...I'm sure you've heard of the famous "Mexican Donkey Show," well the Bahamians have their version of it using the wild cur dogs on the island, which is why they may look like homeless scurvy-laden mutts lying in the street but they've all got smiles on their faces, even when they sleep...

And here's the thing...While repulsive at first, after a few minutes it becomes captivating and before you know it, you're chanting with the crowd, "Give her the knot, Give her the knot!" which in itself will likely fuck you up for the rest of your white bread life...Even more fucked up is the fact that your pants will start to burst, and before you know it you'll think Tevin snuck a candy in your beer and the entire surreal scene is just one fucked up mind bend...It isn't...

Now here's the thing about a Bahamian Doggy Show...If you ever go to one with your significant other, you'll go back to the hotel afterwards and have the best freak pig face sex of your life, you know, the kind the average Eurotrash lesbian has just about every day... The problem here is that you're not with your significant other, oh, that and the fact that your Johnson is thrice engorged and throbbing with the beat of the reggae in the background...So in other words, you're fucked unless you remembered your wallet, which you likely left back at the hotel in case this trip was a scam to rob you of your pitiful collection of traveler's checks...

So there you are with a diamond splitter in your pants and the top 2% of quality exotic dog-fucking Russian pussy in your lap... You'll be ready to pop to the point that you'll start looking at the dogs with your head tilted and that's when you'll catch a view of Macky out of the corner of your eye...Happy fucking Macky just sitting there in the corner with a GoPro helmet cam on his head and those dumb looking sunglasses covering his eyes...It'll hit you like a Tyson left—Sunglasses...And hopefully you brought your extras in your pack...Macky likes him some sunglasses, and you like Sasha and her hand-manicured merkin...So it's a trade out...

Whether you stop or not you'll get back to the hotel in one piece, although in the latter considerably more tattered...Don't say shit about the golden bones or you'll get a visit from the Bille Joe's Posse, which I can assure will make you shit your pants if you even read the words "Golden" or "Bones" in the future, which basically fucks you out of traveling to California and ever hanging out with your

MEXICO RETURNS

stoner buddies again, lest you earn the nickname "Poopsie"...So catch your fish, have a good time, fake an acid high and go back home and tell your buddies what a shithole Freeport is, Mister World Traveler, International Lover, Last Of The Big Time Dog-Fucking Russian Hooker Chasers...

Nicaragua

Nicaragua fly fishing
mjbtrout

Anyone done any fly fishing down in Nicaragua along the Pacific coast or on Lake Nicaragua? Headed down in a week or two looking for some additional intel if anyone has it.

Dood...One of my all time great memories is of being in the shit in Nicaragua with the tracers zipping through the leaves and the howler monkeys throwing scat at the fuckers making all the noise...Touches my cockles, if'n you know what I mean...And it being so close to my heart, I feel obliged to share...

Your timing couldn't be better if you're looking to fish the Roosters or the wahoo bite...If it's marlin you're after then you're about three months late...At least that's the coastal gig...Lake Nicaragua has plenty of muchocka, mojara, Y guapote...Bring a 3 weight and have at it...Me, I'm going coastal...

You'll want to fly in to Managua...Plenty of flights, and don't let all the soldiers walking around on the airfields with machine guns bother you...They're just making sure the little gremmies don't paw you when you get off the plane...See, Nicaragua is a really poor country, and while you wouldn't know it by looking at the people because they're smiling the entire time, if you look close, they have that frozen tooth smile like they took a double tap and haven't fallen down dead yet...It's the chamber of commerce smile at the American enough and he'll eventually throw some Cordoba's your way (although there may be a reach around or humiliating Iphone photography involved)...

Anyway, because they're so poor, they flood the aeropuertos looking for anything they can do to earn a buck..."Carry your rod tubes," senor?... "Need the A-1 Super Pimo taxi," Senor?... "Looking for a sideways vachina," senor? ...Well, you get the picture... Just ignore them and use your hands to part the little booger pickers like Moses parting the Red Sea...

On the south side of the aeropuerto are the Rental Car companies...You want to reserve a car before you go, and let me explain the options...All the major rental car companies are there, and when you look on the Internet, they'll give you the following options: Mini, economy, compact, midsize, standard SUV, standard pickup, standard minivan, full size SUV, Full Size Pickup, Full Size Minivan and premium SUV...And while you may be fluent in Spanish, you may not be fluent in Central American, so let me translate...Mini is a Central American term for Circus Clown Car...Economy means Sardine sized shitbox riding on three wheels and the comical 1/3 wheel spare with in-cab exhaust... Midsize means no back seat...Anything with the word "Standard" before it means "Standard" size for Nicuraguans, which have an average height of a "standard" Labrador Retriever and weigh about the same as a carry-on bag, so figure you and the wife can fit in the Standard four door vehicle as long as one sits in the front and one in the back, and you put anything you brought with you on the roof...Full Size means there's enough room between the roof and your head to wear a hat, as long as it's a ball cap...So you pretty much have to order the Premium SUV, which is the smallest version of the Rav4 in production along with a supercharged 4 cylinder stick shift and sometimes working, sometimes not AC...

NICARAGUA

So, you're welcome ahead of time...

Slide on over to the rental desk, flip the girl behind the counter $4 million Cordobas ($3 American) and tell her you'd like a car without chicken shit on the seat...From there, head southwest for San Juan Del Sur, the land of rocky beaches with crocodiles...And just a side note here, if you need to get rid of a burden (say a wife or gf), you can always tell her you heard there's a beautiful waterfall just up the beach and that she needs to carry a whole chicken there for the waterfall tiki chef to cook up...Crocodiles can smell chicken blood for a thousand yards and you'll notice that the welcome sign with the numbers on it that you can't seem to translate goes up one number afterwards...

San Juan Del Sur is a small coastal village/town with a couple of really nice resorts (they're the buildings with the high walls and guards carrying machine guns) and lots of very nice local hotels/palapas...The local hotels are nice, clean and a lot of them even have windows...Either way, use the mosquito netting...Oh, and don't eat anything with shrimp in it...Ask anyone who's ever come back from Central America with yellow eyes and liver failure and they'll all tell you the same thing, "Don't eat the shrimp," and even if you've had the Heptivac Vaccine, those shrimp have some hepatitis that will scare the shit out of your immunities and anything your dumbass doctor who never made it out of the Managua sideways vagina banister slide and sex show may have prescribed...

Get your room, settle in, then take a walk on the beach...San Juan Del Sur is a big cove with everything based waterfront...On the south end of the cove is a little dive/surf shack that also doubles as a bar with these funky seats that are swings that hang from the ceiling...Look for the longboard on the roof with the donkey riding it...Reef Donkey's is Nora's place, and she has the hookup for the panga wanga, unless of course you want to dole out $1,500 American a day for a tourista boat...Tis up to you...The panga will cost you $50 American, plus they get to keep any fish you catch to feed the town...

MEXICO RETURNS

Grab a swing, order a Diplimatico and pineapple juice and draw little designs in the sand with your feet until Nora rolls up...You'll know Nora from the other girls working there, as she's the one with the obvious European genes...You see, while they're all dark skinned, but there's two main traits to the women of Nicarauga, and only one of them are a beauty...The first type of woman has an Indian influence...She looks like your standard smoking hot Latina babe, only someone has grabbed her by the shoulders and scrunched her body down to the point that she's not fat and not a midget, but she's definitely a fidget...All 3' 11" of her...Now take that girl, grab a pie plate, smash her face in it and rub it around until her head and face are perfectly round, then pull her legs off and put them back on upside down and cake them with dirt to the kneecaps, and you've got the standard Nicaragua Indian influence...Then there's the almond skinned, jet black haired striking, "that is the most beautiful woman I have ever seen, oh wait, no that one is," European Nicaraguan woman...And while the former may have some stellar iguana catching skills, my vote always goes with the 103 pound brown-eyed lap rocket...

Anyway, Nora can line up the Panga...Tell her up front you want to fly fish. Likely you'll end up going out with Gilbert or Edwin, both of whom are very good at the tease and please game...And fuck me running if April isn't the extra super primo wahoo run... So don't even pull your nine weight out of the rod tube...Bring the cannon or you're going to be the Zing-Pow King of lost line and backing on your first fish...Use their flies, they know what works...They tease the fish in using spinning rods and these big fucking pencil poppers that splash like crazy and swim all zig-zaggedy which has the wahoo pissed off and violent with that "Everybody dies" attitude by the time you get the fly in their way...So, you're pretty much going to get bit...

Oh, and a word of caution...Wahoo jump...Particularly when they first feel steel...So before you sting the fish, be sure you know which way it's facing, or you could find yourself jumping overboard with 60 pounds of striped angst chewing "V's" in your camera and rain gear...Also, pay attention to your rod tip, because that initial

112

run is going to blow a head-shaking smoke trail up the side of the boat, and the first time you experience it you're likely going to be standing there stunned like a zit-faced kid who's mom sucked off a roadie to get you a back-stage pass and now you've just learned that Marilyn Manson is a guy look while your reel is going mach 7 and your backing is just starting to slice into the neck of your guide...So keep your tip up, lest you have to figure out how to drive a 22 foot boat 35 feet up onto the sand using your guides head for a paddle...

Now Edwin is a pretty cool cat...your typical funny as shit, I can't understand a word you're saying but I know you're making a joke about that girl's pussy Nicaraguan...Gilbert is more of the sketchimo, ex-Sandinista, kill you for your fancy fishing pliers kind of guy...Or at least that's the air he puts out...Shut that shit down right away...Gilbert grew up in the Hamptons...His dad was a diplomat...Mom was a professional head turner...Which makes Gilbert your standard stoner, underachiever, move back to the mother land and be a part-time fishing guide...And he's a hellofafishingguide...It's the stoner side you have to watch...

The weird thing about Nicaragua is that anything you'd call a "drug" in America is openly sold whether it's legal or not, and if it's not it's only legal until YOU possess it, so always carry a couple of hundred bucks in your shoe...Also, it always comes wrapped in a banana leaf, doesn't matter if it's spliff, whiff, smez or a dollop of hash oil, it's in a tubular green package...So that shit is easy to mix up...About as easy as it was for the Ex-Pat American dickhead tweaker to mix it up in his bathtub...So my suggestion is that you don't try anything Gilbert offers, even an iguana pop...

Just fish your ass off, chill on the ride back, and when you get back to Nora's place pay your guide and flip them a $20 or so, and head back to the hotel. Don't hop in a swing for a post day on the water libation, and definitely don't grab one of those Honduran cigars in the big plastic pretzel tub...Cigars come in boxes or tubes... When they come in pretzel tubs they've been soaking in GHB for three days, which explains the two girls in the swings upside down with burn marks on their lips...They smoked those cigars yesterday...

So take one big puff on that cigar, and then next thing you know, it's piñata mjbtrout holes for everyone...And here's the thing... While Nora may be the single most beautiful woman you've seen in the last 20 minutes, she's also a choker...As in, erotic asphyxiation...As in Gag me out while I'm twitching, and when I wake up I'll return the favor...And there's nothing more pathetic than scrolling through Internet porn at work and seeing yourself in a facesitting video with your legs dancing the spasmodic till you pass our and are thrown on the pile of comatose touristas behind the Reef Donkey...Well, that and the fact that sooner or later those two chicks in the swing are going to wake up...And did I happen to mention that they're not really chicks?...

If you read up on Nicaragua, you'll find the country has one of the highest literacy rates in the world and treats their wimmen worse than their dogs, but they have one of the highest concentrations of plastic surgeons of any country...Cheap plastic surgeons...As in, cheap sex change operation surgeons...As in, fly to Nicaragua for penile removal/ginae reconstruction, but chicken out at the last minute, smoke a GHB chiba and coma out, eventually waking with heavy guilt and the need to define exactly who you are... And the reality here is that most transvestites that have had the estrogen boob growth program and bail on the surgery last minute aren't committed to being women...They're really just bum fuckers...And you being passed out among a pile of losers...Well, you're kind of an easy target...

I guess what I'm trying to say is that Nicaragua is a wonderful country...The fishing is outstanding...The food and drink first rate...The women that are women and have the European influence are beyond beautiful...But the cigars will kill your ass the next day...

Freaks of Nature

Coming to a theatre near you

Part of the philosophy of angling is the pursuit of the biggest, baddest, meanest fish in the water—after all, we all want the trophy we can put on the hood of our car and drive through town. And while big fish come and go, the truly gigantic specimens are those genetic freaks of nature we cross paths with on occasion.

We see the same in humans. There are big guys, and then there's the holy snikey, look at the size of that guy! type who blocks out the sun even though his knuckles drag on the ground. As a rule, there's something squirrelly going down in chromosome town.

And I see the same in fish, and not just through size. Snook have a straight, dark line that runs down their sides, and I've seen that line run down the side, make a complete oval and continue on. I've seen snook with broken lines, incomplete lines, and one that dove to the belly like it was charting the national economy.

Redfish are the classic example of the freckled stepchild. While the majority of the species come with a birthmark, some lack the spot as if daddy was a croaker, while others expand on the concept like Monet with Parkinson's. The largest fish come with a Frankensteinish forehead and shoulders and Halle Berry's waist.

MEXICO RETURNS

When seatrout get big, they look mean, with a pair of fangs that would give Bella Lugosi an eye tic, and the straight-on face of a bullfrog. I guess it's appropriate, since as lunging/grasping predators, when they're feeling froggy, it's time to leap.

On the freshwater side, I've seen mounts of giant bass that were obese to the point of popping, and those that were simply deep but not wide. I'm not sure if either visage was a product of the taxidermist, but the latter would fit well on a book shelf.

One of the most extreme cases of genetic deformity can be seen in dolphin, which already come to the arena sporting a Cro-Magnon forehead that would make a steroid pumping bodybuilder look for height raisers for the seats in his Corvette. Stick a gaff in a 40-pounder, and it just comes naturally to say, "Hey dude, why the long face?" But when you sting a 70-pounder and pull it into the boat, the first thing that comes to mind is that Tyra Banks and the world head-butting champ had a fish baby.

And speaking of high foreheads, the average lookdown comes with a forehead that would make Doogie Howser jealous. Then there's flounder, which have both eyes on the same side of their face, much like an attorney, only with more humility.

Obscenely large great barracuda come with a snaggle-toothed face that looks like they got an overdose of dental growth hormone. It's either that or a long-lasting British influence that will put the Beatles to shame.

Goliath grouper come with a presence of a small van and the intelligence of Jeff Spicoli. They remind me of the chubby kid in school that you'd pick on until he grabbed you in a bear hug and squeezed until your eyeballs bugged out.

I'll hold my tongue when it comes to sawfish, a species that kills its prey with its nose, much like Paris Hilton, only without the 15 minutes of fame. When either of them start swinging their honker in tight quarters, there's an immediate lack of places to hide.

Three species that take on a mutant appearance when they get huge are king mackerel, wahoo and cobia. Kings get deep, wahoo get wide and cobia get blunt like you stood them on their tail and sat on their head as they grew up. When either of these three species hit that gargantuan proportion, it's time to plan out a prearranged landing pad before you sink the gaff. All three come aboard like they want to be in the cockpit, if for no other reason than to test your reflexes as they chase you around the console.

Of all the big fish that spook the hell out of me, the swordfish is the one that makes me think twice about being on the same side of the boat with a big fish that's being landed. Once they lock onto someone with those huge eyes, wherever that person moves becomes the next place for the air to be sliced. A thick, sharp bill swinging wildly doesn't seem bother some people, but the way I figure it, the fish is already pretty peeved about having to catch its meal with its face, so there's no reason to think it's going to whiff at a pitch lobbed over the plate.

Playa del Carmen

Bonefishing advice

A have a cousin that's getting married in Playa del Carmen in the first week of February. I'm spending 5 days there and then venturing off on my own to catch bonefish for another 3-4 days. I recently bought the book, "DIY Bonefishing" by Rod Hamilton, but I'm wondering if anyone has advice on where a guy could spend some time casting for bones (or permit). I have some experience doing this in Belize, but that's about it. I'm maybe one step above rookie status. I can't afford a guide so it will all be DIY. I'd appreciate any help.

Thanks,
TroutBumReinke

First thing you want to know about Playa Del Carmen is that it's a tourist town, which means the locals rob the tourists for a living... Now there are Gringos and Gringos Local, with the latter being the gringos that live there and have an "in"... You can tell the Gringos Local by their hats...They all wear them, which tells the Mexicans to leave them the fuck alone....So the first thing you do when you get to town is find a store that sells sombreros...Get a big ass sombrero, and a pink scarf...Tie the scarf around the base of the sombrero and wear that motherfucker at all times. Even on the beach...All your stuff will be safe at all times and you'll be treated like royalty...Locals discounts everywhere you go, and when you take a taxi, you'll only pay for one person, not a separate fare for every person...In fact, everyone in your party should get sombreros in case you're not together all the time...

Oh, another option…You'll occasionally see someone with a sombrero with a pink scarf and a stuffed parrot on the side…Those are the Hedonists…Sex freaks…Parrot on the right side means you're a pitcher…On the left means a catcher…The stuffed parrot addition is up to you…

So, fishing…

Dude, couple of options here…You could go south to Xcalak, which is about 200 miles and has the rockin' walk-in fishing… But I think Oliver is out of town celebrating his engagement to Beth, and Carter is either filming in the northeast or out in Jackson Hole, so the odds of a pasty-faced gringo getting past the brown tar gang is limited to cash bribes to federales and donkey cart/lookouts…Probably cost you $200 and your watch…If you're lucky…

You could walk-in fish the beach just past the church in San Miguelito, but at a minimum your rental will get jacked…More likely, you'll get jacked along with it, and there's nothing more humiliating than having your clothes cut off with a knife by a guy that less than 5 feet tall while his buddies encourage him with shouts of "apuñalarlo en el culo," which loosely translates into "Stab him in the ass"…

Best option for you would be to make the run up towards Cancun on hwy 307, which is certainly the fastest, but watch for dogs, panthers and dump trucks in the wrong lane…There's a reason most of the rentals have four wheel drive, and it's so you can swerve into the dirt and live, then get back on the road…P.S. It's considered essential to lock your tires and skid on any snakes crossing the road…

About three beers into the drive, you'll come to the first exit you've seen, which is the Punta Nizuc-Cancun shortcut…Take the right…It's a nice two-laner with tropical palm tree foliage in the middle and low desert scrub on either side, so if one of those POS pickups filled with tires loses an axle in front of you, swerve

MEXICO RETURNS

for the sand, not the trees...

You'll go by Wet N' Wild Cancun, swing north along the beach and pass a giant football shaped hotel. About a mile further, you'll see a giant cleared parking lot where the Hotel de Sian was before Hurricane Geoff blew it into the Gulf...On the north end of that empty property and maybe 100 yards up is a dirt road...Take it...It goes to Playa de Piedra...Stone Beach...

The road is only about 1,000 yards long, with 100 of it decent, and the rest just piled rocks from the Aguachille Rio which will be just in sight on your left...Quick word of caution here...The Aquachille River is crystal clear and full of fish...You can see them from the bank...But it's also full of crocodiles...So you might want to forgo the urge to plop a Clouser at the giant school of snappers you can see from the bank...Crocodiles don't have to surface to grab you, and you'll have to step into the water to get away from the bank for a back cast...

Anyway, the path/road ends at Playa de Piedra, this funky hook of a shoreline cove facing southeast with about two miles of beautiful flats...Look down the shoreline and you'll see three palm trees...Start there and wade south...Don't forget your sombrero...You can go all the way to the end of the cove, which would be just norte of the football shaped hotel...About midway, you'll see a small collection of palapas, which is Estaban's Tacoria...Good food, but don't eat any vegetables, as you'll be shitting in a paint can for the next week if you do...

Make sure you have good wading shoes...Bottom is mottled and sharp foot fuckers, with these orange sponges everywhere...They're blood sponges...Step on them, they ink and smear everything, so the bottom of your wading boots will be redish when you're done...They also smell like lavender, so your boots will smell the best they ever have and you'll have that going for you...

Weird thing about Playa de Piedra is that it has a fair amount of current...Fish always feed into the current, so if it's flowing norte, you're golden, but if it's a south current, you'll want to walk all the way to the end of the cove and fish back...I don't know where you're from, but the first thing you'll realize is that Mexico is closer to the equator than you're used to, so it'll be muy caliente...You'll be sweating like a lesbian eating a taco in front of her parents... Don't burn up the one water bottle you brought, you'll need that while fishing...Instead, stop at Esteban's...If it's before 3 p.m., it'll be closed, but someone will be in the hammock under one of the palapa's 24/7...If you're lucky, it'll be Mateo and not Diego...

Mateo is an ex-Long Beach Le Eme, which is the baddest of the baddest Mexican gangsters...His father Manuello was a legend on the coast, but got gunned down by the Columbians back in 02 for helping the company gringos find their camp in Rio Agua- chille...Bad juju there, as it sparked three weeks of pot shots from nowhere at any norte Americano from the Columbians that were holed up along the river...Crocodilles got most of the Columbi- ans, but the locals got the rest...They caught one of the Colum- bians at the mouth of the river trying to float out on a homemade raft, and Diego who was probably 10 or 11 at the time cut off his balls and hung them from a palm tree...That's why it's called Stone Beach...

Despite being covered with tattoos and a Frankenstein scar on his forehead, Mateo is OKAY...Just don't approach him from behind or walk up when he's sleeping...Best thing to do is get about 40 yards away and look for movement...Movement means he's awake...Which is OKAY...It means he just leaned over and picked up a H&K MP5 SD1, which is this little badass machine gun that spits 10 rounds a second...Good thing is it's only got a 30 mag clip...

Mateo will have that in his lap, so NO SUDDEN MOVES... Don't think you'd be the first shooter dressed in plaid with khaki booties and a chest pack to try to take him out...Say very loudly, "Hola Mateo, quiere jugar con las bolas!"...Asking him to play with your balls is the code phrase...When he motions you up, be sure to tell him "Mexico says jalapenos are for pussies"...When you see the smile cross his face, you'll know you're in…See Mateo and I spent a little time together, and one of the things he liked to do was cut up a bunch of jalapenos and not wash his hands… Around noon every day, a dozen or so of the local puntas would wander down to the tacoria looking for a freebie fix, and we'd bet on who would be the last one to run down to the water and squat…Last in, was first up…It's pretty funny to watch…

Now they do sell tacos and other food there, but for the most part, the tacoria is a front for the Goldest of the Gold buds…The REAL Chiba…I mean, two hits and you break out laughing for no reason chiba…Now don't confuse it with the CHEEBA, which is heroin…That shit has a monkey that follows it everywhere, and Mateo knows how I feel about it after Lindy Lude smoked some in a joint and wrecked on the Negro Bridge in a Jeep filled with grenades and we couldn't cross the river for a month…You say "CHEEBA," and he'll think you intercepted the code and are there to take him out…So enunciate C-A-R-E-F-U-L-L-Y… Point to the sombrero…

Mateo speaks good English…Just tell him you want something to drink, and not something with a kick…You just want to hydrate… And not bottled water…That shit is just local water with the caps resealed on them…You want Gatorade or one of the Mexican sodas…Pineapple is my favorite…Drink up a bunch…And then drink some more…It's hot as a mother on those flats…So hot, you'll never take a piss…

If you're lucky, Ramona will be hanging around…You'll know who she is…Not many redheads with tan…She's cool and can fish pretty well…For $40, she'll guide you for four hours on those flats…It's a good deal…Plus, she can carry extra water…She's not bad to look at either…Legs all the way to Miami…She used to be married to one of those world traveling world record chasers who would beat her with his fly rod whenever he broke off a fish…She shot him in Panama about six years ago, and has been Playa de Piedra bound ever since…That's one of the reasons she's always got a 45 on her…Oh, and she LOVES gringos…Doesn't see many there...Usually has to go to town to hook up...So she may come on to you...

Anyway, hydrate, grab Ramona or not and head for the southern end...Don't forget your sombrero...There's a clump of three palm trees (tres palmas) about 60 yards from the dilapidated dock... That's the put-in...Some good sandbars where you'll see the fish coming from 100 yards right away...Mostly small fish, but the occasional five pounder...The bar is hooked like a "C", and on the top is a little clump of rocks with about a four foot drop-off... Permit like that spot...You'll want a white colored crab...Don't fucking strip...Bonk the fish on the head an let it sink...If they follow it down, let it hit bottom and make one long, slow strip... About halfway through the strip you'll feel the fish come tight...

Ramona knows that stuff as well as anyone...And she knows where Twelve O'Clock Rock is...Good permit there too...Most of the shots at bonefish will be singles, pairs or small schools of less than 30...Lead the schools and let them come to the fly...You usually only give it one small strip and you're on...Kinda tough to decide what rod to fish...I like a 6 wt because the bones are so small, but a 'mit will beat your ass on that...An 8 wt is a nice option, and really good if the wind comes up, but you'll be able to waterski some of the smaller bones...7 wt is probably the best of both worlds and helps cast that shitty little weighted crab Ramona likes to tie...(don't tell her I said that)...

Walk and fish, catch a shitpot full of bones and have fun...Around noon you'll hear a lot of music coming from the Tacoria as the puntas show...Watch for the ones running for the water...If you've got a hankering, feel free to walk up and plop in a hammock...Puntas will be all over your sombrero-wearing ass...Keep in mind, the jalapenos...When I first came back to the country it took me three months to get over the "hot ladies"...Asked a girl in Stutgart, Arkansas to put cayenne in her panties once and she bit half my ear off before running for the shower...

Couple of things to keep in mind if you go back to the tacoria...

MEXICO RETURNS

One, these puntas are the high-dollar elites, and while it won't cost you a thing as you're a guest of Mateo, don't let any donkey show humor suggestions slip, or you'll be the donkey's honkey... For a week...Also, if you mess with the puntas after Ramona has already offered a flame job, she might get a little pissed, so don't let her get anywhere near anything you eat or drink, or you'll wake up naked, face down on a table with your manhood sticking through a hole...She's a milker...And you can bet there's going to be some jalapeno hands yanking your unit...And after six or eight rounds of that, you'll have some issues finding that again back home...

Now all this stuff is epic, fish-a-thon, punta-thon unless Diego is in that hammock...Diego is smaller than Mateo, has no scar, but is missing his right foot, which a crocodile bit off while wading those flats, which is the other reason Ramona carries a 45 and is good to have along...If you see a giant brown turd the size of a SUV coming at you underwater, you're already fucked...Then again, If you see a footless Mexican in the hammock, you're also fucked... Literally...Run!...Seriously...Diego is a right sided parrot wearer, and he takes playing with your balls a little more seriously...And the second he sees you, he's thinking, "Batter Up!...

124

Made in the USA
Middletown, DE
11 December 2018